The Writings of Tertullian
Volume III
By Tertullian
This Edition Edited by Anthony Uyl

Devoted Publishing
Woodstock, Ontario, Canada 2017

The Writings of Tertullian - Volume III
By Tertullian (c. 160-c. 230)
This Edition Edited by Anthony Uyl

Originally Edited By Philip Schaff (1819-1893) (Editor)
And Allan Menzies (1845-1916) (Editor)

Originally Published As:
The Writings of the Fathers Down to A.D. 325
Ante-Nicene Fathers Volume 3
Latin Christianity: Its Founder, Tertullian
I. Apologetic; II. Anti-Marcion; III. Ethical

Originally Published By:
T&T Clark, Edinburgh
And WM. B. Eerdmans Publishing Company, Grand Rapids, Michigan

What kind of philosophies do you have?
Let us know!

Visit our online store: www.devotedpublishing.com
Contact us at: devotedpub@hotmail.com
Visit us on Facebook: @DevotedPublishing

Published in Woodstock, Ontario, Canada 2017

For bulk educational rates, please contact us at the above email address.

ISBN: 978-1-77356-158-5

Table of Contents

Part Third

I - On Repentance [8420]

[Translated by the Rev. S. Thelwall.]

Chapter I - Of Heathen Repentance

Repentance, men understand, so far as nature is able, to be an emotion of the mind arising from disgust [8421] at some previously cherished worse sentiment: that kind of men I mean which even we ourselves were in days gone by--blind, without the Lord's light.

From the reason of repentance, however, they are just as far as they are from the Author of reason Himself. Reason, in fact, is a thing of God, inasmuch as there is nothing which God the Maker of all has not provided, disposed, ordained by reason--nothing which He has not willed should be handled and understood by reason. All, therefore, who are ignorant of God, must necessarily be ignorant also of a thing which is His, because no treasure-house [8422] at all is accessible to strangers. And thus, voyaging all the universal course of life without the rudder of reason, they know not how to shun the hurricane which is impending over the world. [8423] Moreover, how irrationally they behave in the practice of repentance, it will be enough briefly to show just by this one fact, that they exercise it even in the case of their good deeds. They repent of good faith, of love, of simple-heartedness, of patience, of mercy, just in proportion as any deed prompted by these feelings has fallen on thankless soil.

They execrate their own selves for having done good; and that species chiefly of repentance which is applied to the best works they fix in their heart, making it their care to remember never again to do a good turn. On repentance for evil deeds, on the contrary, they lay lighter stress. In short, they make this same (virtue) a means of sinning more readily than a means of right-doing.

Chapter II - True Repentance a Thing Divine, Originated by God, and Subject to His Laws

But if they acted as men who had any part in God, and thereby in reason also, they would first weigh well the importance of repentance, and would never apply it in such a way as to make it a ground for convicting themselves of perverse self-amendment. In short, they would regulate the limit of their repentance, because they would reach (a limit) in sinning too--by fearing God, I mean.

But where there is no fear, in like manner there is no amendment; where there is no amendment, repentance is of necessity vain, for it lacks the fruit for which God sowed it; that is, man's salvation. For God--after so many and so great sins of human temerity, begun by the first of the race, Adam, after the condemnation of man, together with the dowry of the world [8424] after his ejection from paradise and subjection to death--when He had hasted back to His own mercy, did from that time onward inaugurate repentance in His own self, by rescinding the sentence of His first wrath, engaging to grant pardon to His own work and image. [8425] And so He gathered together a people for Himself, and fostered them with many liberal distributions of His bounty, and, after so often finding them most ungrateful, ever exhorted them to repentance and sent out the voices of the universal company of the prophets to prophesy. By and by, promising freely the grace which in the last times He was intending to pour as a flood of light on the universal world [8426] through His Spirit, He bade the baptism of repentance lead the way, with the view of first preparing, [8427] by means of the sign and seal of repentance, them whom He was calling, through grace, to (inherit) the promise surely made to Abraham. John holds not his peace, saying, "Enter upon repentance, for now shall salvation approach the nations" [8428] --the Lord, that is, bringing salvation according to God's promise. To Him John, as His harbinger, directed the repentance (which he preached), whose province was the purging of men's minds, that whatever defilement inveterate error had imparted, whatever contamination in the heart of man ignorance had engendered, that repentance should sweep and scrape away, and cast out of doors, and thus prepare the home of the heart, by making it clean, for the Holy Spirit, who was about to supervene, that He might with pleasure introduce Himself there-into, together with His celestial blessings. Of these blessings the title is briefly one-- the salvation of man--the abolition of former sins being the preliminary step. This [8429] is the (final) cause of repentance, this her work, in taking in hand the business of divine mercy. What is profitable to man does service to God.

The rule of repentance, however, which we learn when we know the Lord, retains a definite form,--viz., that no violent hands so to speak, be ever laid on good deeds or thoughts. [8430] For God, never giving His sanction to the reprobation of good deeds, inasmuch as they are His own (of which, being the author, He must necessarily be the defender too), is in like manner the acceptor of them, and if the acceptor, likewise the rewarder. Let, then, the ingratitude of men see to it, [8431] if it attaches repentance even to good works; let their gratitude see to it too, if the desire of earning it be the incentive to well-doing: earthly and mortal are they each. For how small is your gain if you do good to a grateful man! or your loss if to an ungrateful! A good deed has God as its debtor, just as an evil has too; for a judge is rewarder of every cause. Well, since, God as Judge presides over the exacting and maintaining [8432] of justice, which to Him is most dear; and since it is with an eye to justice that He appoints all the sum of His discipline, is there room for doubting that, just as in all our acts universally, so also in the case of repentance, justice must be rendered to God?--which duty can indeed only be fulfilled on the condition that repentance be brought to bear only on sins. Further, no deed but an evil one deserves to be called sin, nor does any one err by well-doing. But if he does not err, why does he invade (the province of) repentance, the private ground of such as do err? Why does he impose on his goodness a duty proper to wickedness? Thus it comes to pass that, when a thing is called into play where it ought not, there, where it ought, it is neglected.

Chapter III - Sins May Be Divided into Corporeal and Spiritual. Both Equally Subject, If Not to Human, Yet to Divine Investigation and Punishment [8433]

What things, then, they be for which repentance seems just and due--that is, what things are to be set down under the head of sin--the occasion indeed demands that I should note down; but (to do so) may seem to be unnecessary. For when the Lord is known, our spirit, having been "looked back upon"[8434] by its own Author, emerges unbidden into the knowledge of the truth; and being admitted to (an acquaintance with) the divine precepts, is by them forthwith instructed that "that from which God bids us abstain is to be accounted sin:"

inasmuch as, since it is generally agreed that God is some great essence of good, of course nothing but evil would be displeasing to good; in that, between things mutually contrary, friendship there is none. Still it will not be irksome briefly to touch upon the fact [8435] that, of sins, some are carnal, that is, corporeal; some spiritual. For since man is composed of this combination of a two-fold substance, the sources of his sins are no other than the sources of his composition. But it is not the fact that body and spirit are two things that constitute the sins mutually different--otherwise they are on this account rather equal, because the two make up one--lest any make the distinction between their sins proportionate to the difference between their substances, so as to esteem the one lighter, or else heavier, than the other: if it be true, (as it is,) that both flesh and spirit are creatures of God; one wrought by His hand, one consummated by His afflatus. Since, then, they equally pertain to the Lord, whichever of them sins equally offends the Lord. Is it for you to distinguish the acts of the flesh and the spirit, whose communion and conjunction in life, in death, and in resurrection, are so intimate, that "at that time" [8436] they are equally raised up either for life or else for judgment; because, to wit, they have equally either sinned or lived innocently? This we would (once for all) premise, in order that we may understand that no less necessity for repentance is incumbent on either part of man, if in anything it have sinned, than on both. The guilt of both is common; common, too, is the Judge--God to wit; common, therefore, is withal the healing medicine of repentance. The source whence sins are named "spiritual" and "corporeal" is the fact that every sin is matter either of act or else of thought: so that what is in deed is "corporeal," because a deed, like a body, is capable of being seen and touched; what is in the mind is "spiritual," because spirit is neither seen nor handled: by which consideration is shown that sins not of deed only, but of will too, are to be shunned, and by repentance purged. For if human finitude [8437] judges only sins of deed, because it is not equal to (piercing) the lurking-places of the will, let us not on that account make light of crimes of the will in God's sight. God is all-sufficient. Nothing from whence any sin whatsoever proceeds is remote from His sight; because He is neither ignorant, nor does He omit to decree it to judgment. He is no dissembler of, nor double-dealer with, [8438] His own clear-sightedness. What (shall we say of the fact) that will is the origin of deed? For if any sins are imputed to chance, or to necessity, or to ignorance, let them see to themselves: if these be excepted, there is no sinning save by will. Since, then, will is the origin of deed, is it not so much the rather amenable to penalty as it is first in guilt? Nor, if some difficulty interferes with its full accomplishment, is it even in that case exonerated; for it is itself imputed to itself: nor; having done the work which lay in its own power, will it be excusable by reason of that miscarriage of its accomplishment. In fact, how does the Lord demonstrate Himself as adding a superstructure to the Law, except by interdicting sins of the will as well (as other sins); while He defines not only the man who had actually invaded another's wedlock to be an adulterer, but likewise him who had contaminated (a woman) by the concupiscence of his gaze? [8439] Accordingly it is dangerous enough for the mind to set before itself what it is forbidden to perform, and rashly through the will to perfect its execution. And since the power of this will is such that, even without fully sating its self-gratification, it stands for a deed; as a deed, therefore, it shall be punished. It is utterly vain to say, "I willed, but yet I did not." Rather you ought to carry the thing through, because you will; or else not to will, because you do not carry it through.

But, by the confession of your consciousness, you pronounce your own condemnation. For if you eagerly desired a good thing, you would have been anxious to carry it through; in like manner, as you do not carry an evil thing through, you ought not to have eagerly desired it. Wherever you take your stand, you are fast bound by guilt; because you have either willed evil, or else have not fulfilled good.

Chapter IV - Repentance Applicable to All the Kinds of Sin. To Be Practised Not Only, Nor Chiefly, for the Good It Brings, But Because God Commands It

To all sins, then, committed whether by flesh or spirit, whether by deed or will, the same God who has destined penalty by means of judgment, has withal engaged to grant pardon by means of repentance, saying to the people, "Repent thee, and I will save thee;" [8440] and again, "I live, saith the Lord, and I will (have) repentance rather than death." [8441] Repentance, then, is "life," since it is preferred to "death." That repentance, O sinner, like myself (nay, rather, less than myself, for pre-eminence in sins I acknowledge to be mine [8442]), do you so hasten to, so embrace, as a shipwrecked man the protection [8443] of some plank. This will draw you forth when sunk in the waves of sins, and will bear you forward into the port of the divine clemency. Seize the opportunity of unexpected felicity: that you, who sometime were in God's sight nothing but "a drop of a bucket," [8444] and "dust of the threshing-floor," [8445] and "a potter's vessel," [8446] may thenceforward become that "tree which is sown beside [8447] the waters, is perennial in leaves, bears fruit at its own time," [8448] and shall not see "fire," [8449] nor "axe." [8450] Having found "the truth," [8451] repent of errors; repent of having loved what God loves not: even we ourselves do not permit our slave-lads not to hate the things which are offensive to us; for the principle of voluntary obedience [8452] consists in similarity of minds.

To reckon up the good, of repentance, the subject-matter is copious, and therefore should be committed to great eloquence. Let us, however, in proportion to our narrow abilities, inculcate one point,--that what God enjoins is good and best. I hold it audacity to dispute about the "good" of a divine precept; for, indeed, it is not the fact that it is good which binds us to obey, but the fact that God has enjoined it. To exact the rendering of obedience the majesty of divine power has the prior[8453] right; the authority of Him who commands is prior to the utility of him who serves. "Is it good to repent, or no?" Why do you ponder? God enjoins; nay, He not merely enjoins, but likewise exhorts. He invites by (offering) reward--salvation, to wit; even by an oath, saying "I live," [8454] He desires that credence may be given Him.

Oh blessed we, for whose sake God swears! Oh most miserable, if we believe not the Lord even when He swears! What, therefore, God so highly commends, what He even (after human fashion) attests on oath, we are bound of course to approach, and to guard with the utmost seriousness; that, abiding permanently in (the faith of) the solemn pledge [8455] of divine grace, we may be able also to persevere in like manner in its fruit [8456] and its benefit.

Chapter V - Sin Never to Be Returned to After Repentance [8457]

For what I say is this, that the repentance which, being shown us and commanded us through God's grace, recalls us to grace [8458] with the Lord, when once learned and undertaken by us ought never afterward to be cancelled by repetition of sin. No pretext of ignorance now remains to plead on your behalf; in that, after acknowledging the Lord, and accepting His precepts [8459] --in short, after engaging in repentance of (past) sins--you again betake yourself to sins. Thus, in as far as you are removed from ignorance, in so far are you cemented [8460] to contumacy. For if the ground on which you had repented of having sinned was that you had begun to fear the Lord, why have you preferred to rescind what you did for fear's sake, except because you have ceased to fear? For there is no other thing but contumacy which subverts fear. Since there is no exception which defends from liability to penalty even such as are ignorant of the Lord--because ignorance of God, openly as He is set before men, and comprehensible as He is even on the score of His heavenly benefits, is not possible [8461] --how perilous is it for Him to be despised when known? Now, that man does despise Him, who, after attaining by His help to an understanding of things good and evil, often an affront to his own understanding--that is, to God's gift--by resuming what he understands ought to be shunned, and what he has already shunned: he rejects the Giver in abandoning the gift; he denies the Benefactor in not honouring the benefit. How can he be pleasing to Him, whose gift is displeasing to himself? Thus he is shown to be not only contumacious toward the Lord, but likewise ungrateful. Besides, that man commits no light sin against the Lord, who, after he had by repentance renounced His rival the devil, and had under this appellation subjected him to the Lord, again upraises him by his own return (to the enemy), and makes himself a ground of exultation to him; so that the Evil One, with his prey recovered, rejoices anew against the Lord. Does he not-- what is perilous even to say, but must be put forward with a view to edification--place the devil before the Lord? For he seems to have made the comparison who has known each; and to have judicially pronounced him to be the better whose (servant) he has preferred again to be. Thus he who, through repentance for sins, had begun to make satisfaction to the Lord, will, through another repentance of his repentance, make satisfaction to the devil, and will be the more hateful to God in proportion as he will be the more acceptable to His rival. But some say that "God is satisfied if He be looked up to with the heart and the mind, even if this be not done in outward act, and that thus they sin without damage to their fear and their faith:"

that is, that they violate wedlock without damage to their chastity; they mingle poison for their parent without damage to their filial duty! Thus, then, they will themselves withal be thrust down into hell without damage to their pardon, while they sin without damage to their fear! Here is a primary example of perversity: they sin, because they fear! [8462] I suppose, if they feared not, they would not sin! Let him, therefore, who would not have God offended not revere Him at all, if fear[8463] is the plea for offending. But these dispositions have been wont to sprout from the seed of hypocrites, whose friendship with the devil is indivisible, whose repentance never faithful.

Chapter VI - Baptism Not to Be Presumptously Received. It Requires Preceding Repentance, Manifested by Amendment of Life

Whatever, then, our poor ability has attempted to suggest with reference to laying hold of repentance once for all, and perpetually retaining it, does indeed bear upon all who are given up to the Lord, as being all competitors for salvation in earning the favour of God; but is chiefly urgent in the case of those young novices who are only just beginning to bedew [8464] their ears with divine discourses, and who, as whelps in yet early infancy, and with eyes not yet perfect, creep about uncertainly, and say indeed that they renounce their former deed, and assume (the profession of) repentance, but neglect to complete it. [8465] For the very end of desiring importunes them to desire somewhat of their former deeds; just as fruits, when they are already beginning to turn into the sourness or bitterness of age, do yet still in some part flatter [8466] their own loveliness. Moreover, a presumptuous confidence in baptism introduces all kind of vicious delay and tergiversation with regard to repentance; for, feeling sure of undoubted pardon of their sins, men meanwhile steal the intervening time, and make it for themselves into a holiday-time [8467] for sinning, rather than a time for learning not to sin. Further, how inconsistent is it to expect pardon of sins (to be granted) to a repentance which they have not fulfilled! This is to hold out your hand for merchandise, but not produce the price.

For repentance is the price at which the Lord has determined to award pardon: He proposes the redemption [8468] of release from penalty at this compensating exchange of repentance. If, then, sellers first examine the coin with which they make their bargains, to see whether it be cut, or scraped, or adulterated, [8469] we believe likewise that the Lord, when about to make us the grant of so costly merchandise, even of eternal life, first institutes a probation of our repentance. "But meanwhile let us defer the reality of our repentance: it will then, I suppose, be clear that we are amended when we are absolved." [8470] By no means; (but our amendment should be manifested) while, pardon being in abeyance, there is still a prospect of penalty; while the penitent does not yet merit--so far as merit we can--his liberation; while God is threatening, not while He is forgiving. For what slave, after his position has been changed by reception of freedom, charges himself with his (past) thefts and desertions?

What soldier, after his discharge, makes satisfaction for his (former) brands? A sinner is bound to bemoan himself before receiving pardon, because the time of repentance is coincident with that of peril and of fear. Not that I deny that the divine benefit--the putting away of sins, I mean--is in every way sure to such as are on the point of entering the (baptismal) water; but what we have to labour for is, that it may be granted us to attain that blessing. For who will grant to you, a man of so faithless repentance, one single sprinkling of any water whatever? To approach it by stealth, indeed, and to get the minister appointed over this business misled by your asseverations, is easy; but God takes foresight for His own treasure, and suffers not the unworthy to steal a march upon it. What, in fact, does He say? "Nothing hid which shall not be revealed." [8471] Draw whatever (veil of) darkness you please over your deeds, "God is light." [8472] But some think as if God were under a necessity of bestowing even on the unworthy, what He has engaged (to give); and they turn His liberality into slavery. But if it is of necessity that God grants us the symbol of death, [8473] then He does so unwillingly. But who permits a gift to be permanently retained which he has granted unwillingly?

For do not many afterward fall out of (grace)? is not this gift taken away from many? These, no doubt, are they who do steal a march upon (the treasure), who, after approaching to the faith of repentance, set up on the sands a house doomed to ruin. Let no one, then, flatter himself on the ground of being assigned to the "recruit-classes" of learners, as if on that account he have a licence even now to sin.

As soon as you "know the Lord," [8474] you should fear Him; as soon as you have gazed on Him, you should reverence Him. But what difference does your "knowing" Him make, while you rest in the same practises as in days bygone, when you knew Him not? What, moreover, is it which distinguishes you from a perfected [8475] servant of God? Is there one Christ for the baptized, another for the learners?

Have they some different hope or reward? some different dread of judgment? some different necessity for repentance? That baptismal washing is a sealing of faith, which faith is begun and is commended by the faith of repentance. We are not washed in order that we may cease sinning, but because we have ceased, since in heart we have been bathed [8476] already. For the first baptism of a learner is this, a perfect fear; [8477] thenceforward, in so far as you have understanding of the Lord faith is sound, the conscience having once for all embraced repentance. Otherwise, if it is (only) after the baptismal waters that we cease sinning, it is of necessity, not of free-will, that we put on innocence. Who, then, is pre-eminent in goodness? he who is not allowed, or he whom it displeases, to be evil? he who is bidden, or he whose pleasure it is, to be free from crime? Let us, then, neither keep our hands from theft unless the hardness of bars withstand us, nor refrain our eyes from the concupiscence of fornication unless we be withdrawn by guardians of our persons, if no one who has surrendered himself to the Lord is to cease sinning unless he be bound thereto by baptism.

But if any entertain this sentiment, I know not whether he, after baptism, do not feel more sadness to think that he has ceased from sinning, than gladness that he hath escaped from it. And so it is becoming that learners desire baptism, but do not hastily receive it: for he who desires it, honours it; he who hastily receives it, disdains it: in the one appears modesty, in the other arrogance; the former satisfies, the latter neglects it; the former covets to merit it, but the latter promises it to himself as a due return; the former takes, the latter usurps it. Whom would you judge worthier, except one who is more amended? whom more amended, except one who is more timid, and on that account has fulfilled the duty of true repentance? for he has feared to continue still in sin, lest he should not merit the reception of baptism. But the hasty receiver, inasmuch as he promised it himself (as his due), being forsooth secure (of obtaining it), could not fear: thus he fulfilled not repentance either, because he lacked the instrumental agent of repentance, that is, fear.[8478] Hasty reception is the portion of irreverence; it inflates the seeker, it despises the Giver. And thus it sometimes deceives, [8479] for it promises to itself the gift before it be due; whereby He who is to furnish the gift is ever offended.

Chapter VII - Of Repentance, in the Case of Such as Have Lapsed After Baptism

So long, Lord Christ, may the blessing of learning or hearing concerning the discipline of repentance be granted to Thy servants, as is likewise behoves them, while learners, [8480] not to sin; in other words, may they thereafter know nothing of repentance, and require nothing of it. It is irksome to append mention of a second--nay, in that case, the last--hope; [8481] lest, by treating of a remedial repenting yet in reserve, we seem to be pointing to a yet further space for sinning.

Far be it that any one so interpret our meaning, as if, because there is an opening for repenting, there were even now, on that account, an opening for sinning; and as if the redundance of celestial clemency constituted a licence for human temerity. Let no one be less good because God is more so, by repeating his sin as often as he is forgiven. Otherwise be sure he will find an end of escaping, when he shall not find one of sinning.

We have escaped once: thus far and no farther let us commit ourselves to perils, even if we seem likely to escape a second time. [8482] Men in general, after escaping shipwreck, thenceforward declare divorce with ship and sea; and by cherishing the memory of the danger, honour the benefit conferred by God,--their deliverance, namely. I praise their fear, I love their reverence; they are unwilling a second time to be a burden to the divine mercy; they fear to seem to trample on the benefit which they have attained; they shun, with a solicitude which at all events is good, to make trial a second time of that which they have once learned to fear. Thus the limit of their temerity is the evidence of their fear.

Moreover, man's fear [8483] is an honour to God. But however, that most stubborn foe (of ours) never gives his malice leisure; indeed, he is then most savage when he fully feels that a man is freed from his clutches; he then flames fiercest while he is fast becoming extinguished. Grieve and groan he must of necessity over the fact that, by the grant of pardon, so many works of death [8484] in man have been overthrown, so many marks of the condemnation which formerly was his own erased. He grieves that that sinner, (now) Christ's servant, is destined to judge him and his angels. [8485] And so he observes, assaults, besieges him, in the hope that he may be able in some way either to strike his eyes with carnal concupiscence, or else to entangle his mind with worldly enticements, or else to subvert his faith by fear of earthly power, or else to wrest him from the sure way by perverse traditions: he is never deficient in stumbling-blocks nor in temptations. These poisons of his, therefore, God foreseeing, although the gate of forgiveness has been shut and fastened up with the bar of baptism, has permitted it still to stand somewhat open. [8486] In the vestibule He has stationed the second repentance for opening to such as knock:

but now once for all, because now for the second time; [8487] but never more because the last time it had been in vain. For is not even this once enough? You have what you now deserved not, for you had lost what you had received. If the Lord's indulgence grants you the means of restoring what you had lost, be thankful for the benefit renewed, not to say amplified; for restoring is a greater thing than giving, inasmuch as having lost is more miserable than never having received at all. However, if any do incur the debt of a second repentance, his spirit is not to be forthwith cut down and undermined by despair. Let it by all means be irksome to sin again, but let not to repent again be irksome: irksome to imperil one's self again, but not to be again set free. Let none be ashamed. Repeated sickness must have repeated medicine. You will show your gratitude to the Lord by not refusing what the Lord offers you. You have offended, but can still be reconciled. You have One whom you may satisfy, and Him willing. [8488]

Chapter VIII - Examples from Scripture to Prove the Lord's Willingness to Pardon

This if you doubt, unravel [8489] the meaning of "what the Spirit saith to the churches." [8490] He imputes to the Ephesians "forsaken love;" [8491] reproaches the Thyatirenes with "fornication," and "eating of things sacrificed to idols;" [8492] accuses the Sardians of "works not full;" [8493] censures the Pergamenes for teaching perverse things; [8494] upbraids the Laodiceans for trusting to their riches; [8495] and yet gives them all general monitions to repentance--under comminations, it is true; but He would not utter comminations to one unrepentant if He did not forgive the repentant. The matter were doubtful if He had not withal elsewhere demonstrated this profusion of His clemency. Saith He not, [8496] "He who hath fallen shall rise again, and he who hath been averted shall be converted?" He it is, indeed, who "would have mercy rather than sacrifices." [8497] The heavens, and the angels who are there, are glad at a man's repentance. [8498] Ho! you sinner, be of good cheer! you see where it is that there is joy at your return.

What meaning for us have those themes of the Lord's parables? Is not the fact that a woman has lost a drachma, and seeks it and finds it, and invites her female friends to share her joy, an example of a restored sinner? [8499] There strays, withal, one little ewe of the shepherd's; but the flock was not more dear than the one: that one is earnestly sought; the one is longed for instead of all; and at length she is found, and is borne back on the shoulders of the shepherd himself; for much had she toiled [8500] in straying. [8501] That most gentle father, likewise, I will not pass over in silence, who calls his prodigal son home, and willingly receives him repentant after his indigence, slays his best fatted calf, and graces his joy with a banquet. [8502] Why not?

He had found the son whom he had lost; he had felt him to be all the dearer of whom he had made a gain. Who is that father to be understood by us to be?

God, surely: no one is so truly a Father; [8503] no one so rich in paternal love. He, then, will receive you, His own son, [8504] back, even if you have squandered what you had received from Him, even if you return naked--just because you have returned; and will joy more over your return than over the sobriety of the other; [8505] but only if you heartily repent--if you compare your own hunger with the plenty of your Father's "hired servants"--if you leave behind you the swine, that unclean herd--if you again seek your Father, offended though He be, saying, "I have sinned, nor am worthy any longer to be called Thine."

Confession of sins lightens, as much as dissimulation aggravates them; for confession is counselled by (a desire to make) satisfaction, dissimulation by contumacy.

Chapter IX - Concerning the Outward Manifestations by Which This Second Repentance is to Be Accompanied

The narrower, then, the sphere of action of this second and only (remaining) repentance, the more laborious is its probation; in order that it may not be exhibited in the conscience alone, but may likewise be carried out in some (external) act. This act, which is more usually expressed and commonly spoken of under a Greek name, is ἐξομολόγησις , [8506] whereby we confess our sins to the Lord, not indeed as if He were ignorant of them, but inasmuch as by confession satisfaction is settled,[8507] of confession repentance is born; by repentance God is appeased. And thus ἐξομολόγησις is a discipline for man's prostration and humiliation, enjoining a demeanor calculated to move mercy. With regard also to the very dress and food, it commands (the penitent) to lie in sackcloth and ashes, to cover his body in mourning, [8508] to lay his spirit low in sorrows, to exchange for severe treatment the sins which he has committed; moreover, to know no food and drink but such as is plain,--not for the stomach's sake, to wit, but the soul's; for the most part, however, to feed prayers on fastings, to groan, to weep and make outcries [8509] unto the Lord your [8510] God; to bow before the feet of the presbyters, and kneel to God's dear ones; to enjoin on all the brethren to be ambassadors to bear his [8511] deprecatory supplication (before God).

All this ἐξομολόγησις (does), that it may enhance repentance; may honour God by its fear of the (incurred) danger; may, by itself pronouncing against the sinner, stand in the stead of God's indignation, and by temporal mortification (I will not say frustrate, but) expunge eternal punishments. Therefore, while it abases the man, it raises him; while it covers him with squalor, it renders him more clean; while it accuses, it excuses; while it condemns, it absolves. The less quarter you give yourself, the more (believe me) will God give you.

Chapter X - Of Men's Shrinking from This Second Repentance and ἐξομολόγησις, and of the Unreasonableness of Such Shrinking

Yet most men either shun this work, as being a public exposure [8512] of themselves, or else defer it from day to day. I presume (as being) more mindful of modesty than of salvation; just like men who, having contracted some malady in the more private parts of the body, avoid the privity of physicians, and so perish with their own bashfulness. It is intolerable, forsooth, to modesty to make satisfaction to the offended Lord! to be restored to its forfeited [8513] salvation! Truly you are honourable in your modesty; bearing an open forehead for sinning, but an abashed one for deprecating! I give no place to bashfulness when I am a gainer by its loss; when itself in some son exhorts the man, saying, "Respect not me; it is better that I perish through [8514] you, i.e. than you through me." At all events, the time when (if ever) its danger is serious, is when it is a butt for jeering speech in the presence of insulters, where one man raises himself on his neighbour's ruin, where there is upward clambering over the prostrate.

But among brethren and fellow-servants, where there is common hope, fear, [8515] joy, grief, suffering, because there is a common Spirit from a common Lord and Father, why do you think these brothers to be anything other than yourself? Why flee from the partners of your own mischances, as from such as will derisively cheer them? The body cannot feel gladness at the trouble of any one member, [8516] it must necessarily join with one consent in the grief, and in labouring for the remedy. In a company of two [8517] is the church; [8518] but the church is Christ.[8519] When, then, you cast yourself at the brethren's knees, you are handling Christ, you are entreating Christ. In like manner, when they shed tears over you, it is Christ who suffers, Christ who prays the Father for mercy. What a son [8520] asks is ever easily obtained. Grand indeed is the reward of modesty, which the concealment of our fault promises us! to wit, if we do hide somewhat from the knowledge of man, shall we equally conceal it from God? Are the judgment of men and the knowledge of God so put upon a par?

Is it better to be damned in secret than absolved in public? But you say, "It is a miserable thing thus to come to ἐξομολόγησις:" yes, for evil does bring to misery; but where repentance is to be made, the misery ceases, because it is turned into something salutary. Miserable it is to be cut, and cauterized, and racked with the pungency of some (medicinal) powder: still, the things which heal by unpleasant means do, by the benefit of the cure, excuse their own offensiveness, and make present injury bearable for the sake [8521] of the advantage to supervene.

Chapter XI - Further Strictures on the Same Subject

What if, besides the shame which they make the most account of, men dread likewise the bodily inconveniences; in that, unwashen, sordidly attired, estranged from gladness, they must spend their time in the roughness of sackcloth, and the horridness of ashes, and the sunkenness of face caused by fasting? Is it then becoming for us to supplicate for our sins in scarlet and purple?

Hasten hither with the pin for panning the hair, and the powder for polishing the teeth, and some forked implement of steel or brass for cleaning the nails. Whatever of false brilliance, whatever of feigned redness, is to be had, let him diligently apply it to his lips or cheeks. Let him furthermore seek out baths of more genial temperature in some gardened or seaside retreat; let him enlarge his expenses; let him carefully seek the rarest delicacy of fatted fowls; let him refine his old wine: and when any shall ask him, "On whom are you lavishing all this?" let him say, "I have sinned against God, and am in peril of eternally perishing: and so now I am drooping, and wasting and torturing myself, that I may reconcile God to myself, whom by sinning I have offended." Why, they who go about canvassing for the obtaining of civil office, feel it neither degrading nor irksome to struggle, in behalf of such their desires, with annoyances to soul and body; and not annoyances merely, but likewise contumelies of all kinds. What meannesses of dress do they not affect? what houses do they not beset with early and late visits?--bowing whenever they meet any high personage, frequenting no banquets, associating in no entertainments, but voluntarily exiled from the felicity of freedom and festivity: and all that for the sake of the fleeting joy of a single year! Do we hesitate, when eternity is at stake, to endure what the competitor for consulship or prætorship puts up with? [8522] and shall we be tardy in offering to the offended Lord a self-chastisement in food and raiment, which [8523] Gentiles lay upon themselves when they have offended no one at all? Such are they of whom Scripture makes mention: "Woe to them who bind their own sins as it were with a long rope." [8524]

Chapter XII - Final Considerations to Induce to ἐξομολόγησις

If you shrink back from ἐξομολόγησις, consider in your heart the hell, [8525] which ἐξομολόγησις will extinguish for you; and imagine first the magnitude of the penalty, that you may not hesitate about the adoption of the remedy. What do we esteem that treasure-house of eternal fire to be, when small vent-holes [8526] of it rouse such blasts of flames that neighbouring cities either are already no more, or are in daily expectation of the same fate? The haughtiest [8527] mountains start asunder in the birth-throes of their inly-gendered fire; and--which proves to us the perpetuity of the judgment--though they start asunder, though they be devoured, yet come they never to an end. Who will not account these occasional punishments inflicted on the mountains as examples of the judgment which menaces the impenitent? Who will not agree that such sparks are but some few missiles and sportive darts of some inestimably vast centre of fire? Therefore, since you know that after the first bulwarks of the Lord's baptism [8528] there still remains for you, in ἐξομολόγησις a second reserve of aid against hell, why do you desert your own salvation? Why are you tardy to approach what you know heals you?

Even dumb irrational animals recognise in their time of need the medicines which have been divinely assigned them. The stag, transfixed by the arrow, knows that, to force out the steel, and its inextricable lingerings, he must heal himself with dittany. The swallow, if she blinds her young, knows how to give them eyes again by means of her own swallow-wort. [8529] Shall the sinner, knowing that ἐξομολόγησις has been instituted by the Lord for his restoration, pass that by which restored the Babylonian king [8530] to his realms? Long time had he offered to the Lord his repentance, working out his ἐξομολόγησις by a seven years' squalor, with his nails wildly growing after the eagle's fashion, and his unkempt hair wearing the shagginess of a lion. Hard handling! Him whom men were shuddering at, God was receiving back. But, on the other hand, the Egyptian emperor--who, after pursuing the once afflicted people of God, long denied to their Lord, rushed into the battle [8531] --did, after so many warning plagues, perish in the parted sea, (which was permitted to be passable to "the People" alone,) by the backward roll of the waves: [8532] for repentance and her handmaid [8533] ἐξομολόγησις he had cast away.

Why should I add more touching these two planks [8534] (as it were) of human salvation, caring more for the business of the pen [8535] than the duty of my conscience? For, sinner as I am of every dye, [8536] and born for nothing save repentance, I cannot easily be silent about that concerning which also the very head and fount of the human race, and of human offence, Adam, restored by ἐξομολόγησις to his own paradise, [8537] is not silent.

Elucidations

I.

(Such as have lapsed, cap. vii)

The penitential system of the Primitive days, referred to in our author, began to be changed when less public confessions were authorized, on account of the scandals which publicity generated. Changes were as follows:

1. A grave presbyter was appointed to receive and examine voluntary penitents as the Penitentiary of a diocese, and to suspend or reconcile them with due solemnities--circa a.d. 250.

2. This plan also became encumbered with difficulties and was abolished in the East, circa a.d. 400.

3. A discipline similar to that of the Anglican Church (which is but loosely maintained therein) succeeded, under St. Chrysostom; who frequently maintains the sufficiency of confession according to Matt. vi. 6. A Gallican author [8538] says--"this is the period regarded by historians as the most brilliant in Church history. At the close of the fourth century, in the great churches of the Orient, sixty thousand Christians received the Eucharistic communion, in one day, in both kinds, with no other than their private confessions to Almighty God. The scandalous evil-liver alone was repelled from the Eucharistic Table." This continued till circa a.d. 700.

4. Particular, but voluntary confessions were now made in the East and West, but with widely various acceptance under local systems of discipline. The absolutions were precatory: "may God absolve Thee." This lasted, even in the West, till the compulsory system of the Lateran Council, a.d. 1215.

5. Since this date, so far as the West is concerned, the whole system of corrupt casuistry and enforced confession adopted in the West has utterly destroyed the Primitive doctrine and discipline as to sin and its remedy wherever it prevails. In the East, private confession exists in a system wholly different and one which maintains the Primitive Theology and the Scriptural principle. (1) It is voluntary; (2) it is free from the corrupt system of the casuists; (3) it distinguishes between Ecclesiastical Absolution and that of Him who alone "seeth in secret;" (4) it admits no compromise with attrition, but exacts the contrite heart and the firm resolve to go and sin no more, and (5) finally, it employs a most guarded and Evangelical formula of remission, of which see Elucidation IV.

II.

(The last hope, cap. vii)

How absolutely the Lateran Council has overthrown the Primitive discipline is here made manifest. The spirit of the latter is expressed by our author in language which almost prompts to despair. It makes sin "exceeding sinful" and even Ecclesiastical forgiveness the reverse of easy.

The Lateran System of enforced Confession makes sin easy and restoration to a sinless state equally so: a perpetual resort to the confessor being the only condition for evil living, and a chronic state of pardon and peace.

But, let the Greek Church be heard in this matter, rather than an Anglican Catholic. I refer to Macarius, Bishop of Vinnitza and Rector of the Theological Academy of St. Petersburg, as follows:[8539] "It is requisite (for the effective reception of Absolution) at least according to the teaching of the Orthodox Church of the Orient, that the following conditions be observed: (1) Contrition for sins, is in the very nature of Penitence, indispensable; (2), consequently, there must be a firm resolution to reform the life; (3) also, faith in Christ and hope in his mercy, with (4) auricular confession before the priest." He allows that this latter condition was not primitive, but was a maternal concession to penitents of later date: this, however, is voluntary, and of a widely different form from that of the Latin, as will appear below in Elucidation IV.

Now, he contrasts with this the system of Rome, and condemns it, on overwhelming considerations.

1. It makes penances compensations [8540] or "satisfaction," offered for sins to divine Justice, this (he says) "is in contradiction with the Christian doctrine of justification, the Scripture teaching one full and entire satisfaction for the sins of the whole human race, once for all presented by our Lord Jesus Christ. This doctrine is equally in conflict with the entire teaching of the Primitive Church."

2. It introduces a false system of indulgences, as the consequence of its false premises.

3. He demonstrates the insufficiency of attrition, which respects the fear of punishment, and not sin itself. But the Council of Trent affirms the sufficiency of attrition, and permits the confessor to absolve the attrite.

Needless to say, the masses accept this wide gate and broad way to salvation rather than the strait gate and narrow way of hating sin and reforming the life, in obedience to the Gospel.

III.

(Among brethren, cap. x)

A controversial writer has lately complained that Bp. Kaye speaks of the public confession treated of by our author in this work, and adds--"Tertullian nowhere used the word public." The answer is that he speaks of the discipline of ἐξομολόγησις, which was, in its own nature, as public as preaching. A Gallican writer, less inclined to Jesuitism in the use of words, says frankly: "When one studies this question, with the documents before his eyes, it is impossible not to confess that the Primitive discipline of the Church exhibits not a vestige of the auricular confession afterwards introduced." See Irenæus, Adv. Hæres. Vol. I. p. 335, this Series. The Lii. of the canons called Apostolical, reflects a very simple view of the matter, in these words: "If any Bishop or Presbyter will not receive one who turns from his sins, but casts him out, let him be deposed: for he grieves Christ, who said, There shall be joy in heaven over one sinner that repenteth." The ascetic spirit of our author seems at war with that of this Canon.

IV.

(ἐξομολόγησις, cap. xii)

To this day, in the Oriental Churches, the examination of the presbyter who hears the voluntary confession of penitents, is often very primitive in its forms and confined to general inquiries under the Decalogue. The Casuistry of (Dens and Liguori) the Western Schemata Practica has not defiled our Eastern brethren to any great extent.

In the office [8541] (᾿Ακολουθία τῶν ἐξομολουγουμένων) we have a simple and beautiful form of prayer and supplication in which the following is the formula of Absolution: "My Spiritual child, who hast confessed to my humility, I, unworthy and a sinner, have not the power to forgive sins on Earth; God only can: and through that Divine voice which came to the Apostles, after the Resurrection of our Lord Jesus Christ, saying--Whosoever sins, etc.,' we, therein confiding, say-- Whatsoever thou hast confessed to my extreme humility, and whatsoever thou hast omitted to say, either through ignorance or forgetfulness, God forgive thee in this present world and in that which is to come."

The plural (We therein confiding) is significant and a token of Primitive doctrine: i.e. of confession before the whole Church, (2 Cor. ii. 10): and note the precatory form--"God forgive thee." The perilous form Ego te absolvo is not Catholic: it dates from the thirteenth century and is used in the West only. It is not wholly dropped from the Anglican Office, but has been omitted from the American Prayer-Book.

Footnotes:

8420. [We pass from the polemical class of our author's writings to those of a practical and ethical character. This treatise on Penitence is the product of our author's best days, and may be dated a.d. 192.]

8421. "Offensa sententiæ pejoris;" or possibly, "the miscarriage of some," etc.

8422. Thesaurus.

8423. Sæculo. [Erasmus doubted the genuineness of this treatise, partly because of the comparative purity of its style. See Kaye, p. 42.]

8424. Sæculi dote. With which he had been endowed. Comp. Gen. i. 28; Ps. viii. 4-8.

8425. i.e., man.

8426. Orbi.

8427. Componeret.

8428. Comp. Matt. iii. 1, 2; Mark i. 4; Luke iii. 4-6.

8429. i.e., man's salvation.

8430. See the latter part of c. i.

8431. Viderit.

8432. Or, "defending."

8433. [Without reference to Luther's theory of justification, we must all adopt this as the test of "a standing or falling church," viz. "How does it deal with sin and the sinner."]

8434. Luke xxii. 61.

8435. Or, "briefly to lay down the rule."

8436. i.e., in the judgment-day. Compare the phrase "that day and that hour" in Scripture.

8437. Mediocritas.

8438. Prævaricatorem: comp. ad Ux.b. ii. c. ii. ad init.

8439. Matt. v. 27, 28; comp. de Idol. ii.

8440. Comp. Ezek. xviii. 30, 32.

8441. The substance of this is found in Ezek. xxxiii. 11.

8442. Compare 1 Tim. i. 16.

8443. Comp. c. xii. sub fin.
[Ut naufragus alicuius tabulæ fidem; this expression soon passed into Theological technology, and as "the plank after shipwreck" is universally known.]

8444. Isa. xl. 15.

8445. Dan. ii. 35; Matt. iii. 12.

8446. Ps. ii. 9; Rev. ii. 27.

8447. Penes.

8448. Ps. i. 3; Jer. xvii. 8. Compare Luke xxiii. 31.

8449. Jer. xvii. 8; Matt. iii. 10.

8450. Matt. iii. 10.

8451. John xiv. 6.

8452. Obsequii.

8453. Or, "paramount."

8454. See ref. 1 on the preceding page. The phrase is "as I live" in the English version.

8455. "Asseveratione:" apparently a play on the word, as compared with "perseverare," which follows.

8456. Or, "enjoyment."

8457. [The formidable doctrine of 1 John iii. 9; v. 18, etc. must excuse our author for his severe adherence to this principle of purifying the heart from habitual sin. But, the church refused to press it against St. Matt. xviii. 22. In our own self-indulgent day, we are more prone, I fear, to presumption than to over strictness. The Roman casuists make attrition suffice, and so turn absolution into a mere sponge, and an encouragement to perpetual sinning and formal confession.]

8458. i.e., favour.

8459. Which is solemnly done in baptism.

8460. Adglutinaris.

8461. Acts xiv. 15-17: "licet" here may ="lawful," "permissible," "excusable."

8462. "Timent," not "metuunt." "Metus" is the word Tertullian has been using above for religious, reverential fear.

8463. Timor.

8464. Deut. xxxii. 2.

8465. i.e., by baptism.

8466. Adulantur.

8467. "Commeatus," a military word ="furlough," hence "holiday-time."

8468. i.e., repurchase.

8469. Adulter; see de Idol. c. i.

8470. i.e., in baptism.

8471. Luke viii. 17.

8472. 1 John i. 5.

8473. Symbolum mortis indulget. Comp. Rom. vi. 3, 4, 8; Col. ii. 12, 20.

8474. Jer. xxxi. (LXX. xxxviii.) 34; Heb. viii. 11.

8475. i.e., in baptism.

8476. See John xiii. 10 and Matt. xxiii. 26.

8477. Metus integer.

8478. Metus.

8479. Or, "disappoints," i.e., the hasty recipient himself.

8480. i.e., before baptism.

8481. [Elucidation I. See infra, this chapter, sub fine.]

8482. [When our author wrote to the Martyrs, (see cap. 1.) he was less disposed to such remorseless discipline: and perhaps we have here an element of his subsequent system, one which led him to accept the discipline of Montanism. On this general subject, we shall find enough when we come to Cyprian and Novatian.]

8483. Timor.

8484. "Mortis opera," or "deadly works:" cf. de Idol. c. iv. (mid.), "perdition of blood," and the note there.

8485. 1 Cor. vi. 3.

8486. Or, "has permitted somewhat still to stand open."

8487. [See cap. vii. supra.]

8488. To accept the satisfaction.

8489. Evolve: perhaps simply ="read."

8490. Rev. ii. 7, 11, 17, 29; iii. 6, 13, 21.

8491. Rev. ii. 4.

8492. Rev. ii. 20.

8493. Rev. iii. 2.

8494. Rev. ii. 14, 15.

8495. Rev. iii. 17.

8496. Jer. viii. 4 (in LXX.) appears to be the passage meant. The Eng. Ver. is very different.

8497. Hos. vi. 6; Matt. ix. 13. The words in Hosea in the LXX. are, διότι ἔλεος θέλω ἢ θυσίαν (al. καὶ οὐ θυσίαν).

8498. Luke xv. 7, 10.

8499. Luke xv. 8-10.

8500. Or, "suffered."

8501. Luke xv. 3-7.

8502. Luke xv. 11-32.

8503. Cf. Matt. xxiii. 9; and Eph. iii. 14, 15, in the Greek.

8504. Publicly enrolled as such in baptism; for Tertullian here is speaking solely of the "second repentance."

8505. See Luke xv. 29-32.

8506. Utter confession.

8507. For the meaning of "satisfaction," see Hooker Eccl. Pol. vi. 5, where several references to the present treatise occur. [Elucidation II.]

8508. Sordibus.

8509. Cf. Ps. xxii. 1 (in LXX. xxii. 3), xxxviii. 8 (in the LXX. xxxvii. 9). Cf. Heb. v. 7.

8510. Tertullian changes here to the second person, unless Oehler's "tuum" be a misprint for "suum."

8511. "Suæ," which looks as if the "tuum" above should be "suum." [St. James v. 16.]

8512. [Elucidation III.]

8513. Prodactæ.

8514. Per. But "per," according to

Oehler, is used by Tertullian as ="propter" --on your account, for your sake.

8515. Metus.

8516. 1 Cor. xii. 26.

8517. In uno et altero.

8518. See Matt. xviii. 20.

8519. i.e. as being His body.

8520. Or, "the Son." Comp. John xi. 41, 42.

8521. Or, "by the grace."

8522. Quod securium virgarumque petitio sustinet.

8523. "Quæ," neut. pl.

8524. Isa. v. 18 (comp. the LXX.).

8525. Gehennam. Comp. ad Ux.ii. c. vi. ad fin.

8526. Fumariola, i.e. the craters of volcanoes.

8527. Superbissimi: perhaps a play on the word, which is connected with "super" and "superus," as "haughty" with "high."

8528. For Tertullian's distinction between "the Lord's baptism" and "John's" see de Bapt. x.

8529. Or "celandine," which is perhaps only another form of "chelidonia" ("Chelidonia major," Linn.).

8530. Dan. iv. 25 sqq. See de Pa. xiii.

8531. Proelium.

8532. Ex. xiv. 15-31.

8533. "Ministerium," the abstract for the concrete: so "servitia" = slaves.

8534. See c. iv. [Tabula was the word in cap. iv. but here it becomes planca, and planca post naufragium is the theological formula, ever since, among Western theologians.]

8535. See de Bapt. xii. sub init.

8536. Lit. "of all brands." Comp. c. vi.: "Does the soldier...make satisfaction for his brands."

8537. Cf. Gen. iii. 24 with Luke xxiii. 43, 2 Cor. xii. 4, and Rev. ii. 7. [Elucidation IV.]

8538. Le Confesseur, par L'Abbé * * * p. 15, Brussels 1866.

8539. Theol. Dogmat. Orthodoxe, pp. 529-541, etc.

8540. Couc. Trident. Sess. xiv. cap. 8.

8541. The Great Euchologion, p. 220, Venice, 1851.

II - On Baptism

[Translated by the Rev. S. Thelwall.]

Chapter I - Introduction. Origin of the Treatise

Happy is our [8542] sacrament of water, in that, by washing away the sins of our early blindness, we are set free and admitted into eternal life! A treatise on this matter will not be superfluous; instructing not only such as are just becoming formed (in the faith), but them who, content with having simply believed, without full examination of the grounds [8543] of the traditions, carry (in mind), through ignorance, an untried though probable faith. The consequence is, that a viper of the Cainite heresy, lately conversant in this quarter, has carried away a great number with her most venomous doctrine, making it her first aim to destroy baptism. Which is quite in accordance with nature; for vipers and asps and basilisks themselves generally do affect arid and waterless places. But we, little fishes, after the example of our ΙΧΘΥΣ [8544] Jesus Christ, are born in water, nor have we safety in any other way than by permanently abiding in water; so that most monstrous creature, who had no right to teach even sound doctrine, [8545] knew full well how to kill the little fishes, by taking them away from the water!

Chapter II - The Very Simplicity of God's Means of Working, a Stumbling-Block to the Carnal Mind

Well, but how great is the force of perversity for so shaking the faith or entirely preventing its reception, that it impugns it on the very principles of which the faith consists! There is absolutely nothing which makes men's minds more obdurate than the simplicity of the divine works which are visible in the act, when compared with the grandeur which is promised thereto in the effect; so that from the very fact, that with so great simplicity, without pomp, without any considerable novelty of preparation, finally, without expense, a man is dipped in water, and amid the utterance of some few words, is sprinkled, and then rises again, not much (or not at all) the cleaner, the consequent attainment of eternity [8546] is esteemed the more incredible. I am a deceiver if, on the contrary, it is not from their circumstance, and preparation, and expense, that idols' solemnities or mysteries get their credit and authority built up. Oh, miserable incredulity, which quite deniest to God His own properties, simplicity and power! What then?

Is it not wonderful, too, that death should be washed away by bathing? But it is the more to be believed if the wonderfulness be the reason why it is not believed. For what does it behove divine works to be in their quality, except that they be above all wonder? [8547] We also ourselves wonder, but it is because we believe. Incredulity, on the other hand, wonders, but does not believe: for the simple acts it wonders at, as if they were vain; the grand results, as if they were impossible. And grant that it be just as you think [8548] sufficient to meet each point is the divine declaration which has forerun: "The foolish things of the world hath God elected to confound its wisdom;"[8549] and, "The things very difficult with men are easy with God." [8550] For if God is wise and powerful (which even they who pass Him by do not deny), it is with good reason that He lays the material causes of His own operation in the contraries of wisdom and of power, that is, in foolishness and impossibility; since every virtue receives its cause from those things by which it is called forth.

Chapter III - Water Chosen as a Vehicle of Divine Operation and Wherefore. Its Prominence First of All in Creation

Mindful of this declaration as of a conclusive prescript, we nevertheless proceed to treat the question, "How foolish and impossible it is to be formed anew by water. In what respect, pray, has this material substance merited an office of so high dignity?" The authority, I suppose, of the liquid element has to be examined. [8551] This [8552] however, is found in abundance, and that from the very beginning. For water is one of those things which, before all the furnishing of the world, were quiescent with God in a yet unshapen [8553] state. "In the first beginning," saith Scripture, "God made the heaven and the earth. But the earth was invisible, and unorganized, [8554] and darkness was over the abyss; and the Spirit of the Lord was hovering [8555] over the waters." [8556] The first thing, O man, which you have to venerate, is the age of the waters in that their substance is ancient; the second, their dignity, in that they were the seat of the Divine Spirit, more pleasing to Him, no doubt, than all the other then existing elements. For the darkness was total thus far, shapeless, without the ornament of stars; and the abyss gloomy; and the earth unfurnished; and the heaven unwrought: water [8557] alone--always a perfect, gladsome, simple material substance, pure in itself--supplied a worthy vehicle to God.

What of the fact that waters were in some way the regulating powers by which the disposition of the world thenceforward was constituted by God?

For the suspension of the celestial firmament in the midst He caused by "dividing the waters;"[8558] the suspension of "the dry land" He accomplished by "separating the waters." After the world had been hereupon set in order through its elements, when inhabitants were given it, "the waters" were the first to receive the precept "to bring forth living creatures." [8559] Water was the first to produce that which had life, that it might be no wonder in baptism if waters know how to give life. [8560] For was not the work of fashioning man himself also achieved with the aid of waters?

Suitable material is found in the earth, yet not apt for the purpose unless it be moist and juicy; which (earth) "the waters," separated the fourth day before into their own place, temper with their remaining moisture to a clayey consistency. If, from that time onward, I go forward in recounting universally, or at more length, the evidences of the "authority" of this element which I can adduce to show how great is its power or its grace; how many ingenious devices, how many functions, how useful an instrumentality, it affords the world, I fear I may seem to have collected rather the praises of water than the reasons of baptism; although I should thereby teach all the more fully, that it is not to be doubted that God has made the material substance which He has disposed throughout all His products[8561] and works, obey Him also in His own peculiar sacraments; that the material substance which governs terrestrial life acts as agent likewise in the celestial.

Chapter IV - The Primeval Hovering of the Spirit of God Over the Waters Typical of Baptism. The Universal Element of Water Thus Made a Channel of Sanctification. Resemblance Between the Outward Sign and the Inward Grace

But it will suffice to have thus called at the outset those points in which withal is recognised that primary principle of baptism,--which was even then fore-noted by the very attitude assumed for a type of baptism,--that the Spirit of God, who hovered over (the waters) from the beginning, would continue to linger over the waters of the baptized. [8562] But a holy thing, of course, hovered over a holy; or else, from that which hovered over that which was hovered over borrowed a holiness, since it is necessary that in every case an underlying material substance should catch the quality of that which overhangs it, most of all a corporeal of a spiritual, adapted (as the spiritual is) through the subtleness of its substance, both for penetrating and insinuating. Thus the nature of the waters, sanctified by the Holy One, itself conceived withal the power of sanctifying. Let no one say, "Why then, are we, pray, baptized with the very waters which then existed in the first beginning?" Not with those waters, of course, except in so far as the genus indeed is one, but the species very many. But what is an attribute to the genus reappears [8563] likewise in the species. And accordingly it makes no difference whether a man be washed in a sea or a pool, a stream or a fount, a lake or a trough;[8564]

nor is there any distinction between those whom John baptized in the Jordan and those whom Peter baptized in the Tiber, unless withal the eunuch whom Philip baptized in the midst of his journeys with chance water, derived (therefrom) more or less of salvation than others.[8565] All waters, therefore, in virtue of the pristine privilege of their origin, do, after invocation of God, attain the sacramental power of sanctification; for the Spirit immediately supervenes from the heavens, and rests over the waters, sanctifying them from Himself; and being thus sanctified, they imbibe at the same time the power of sanctifying. Albeit the similitude may be admitted to be suitable to the simple act; that, since we are defiled by sins, as it were by dirt, we should be washed from those stains in waters. But as sins do not show themselves in our flesh (inasmuch as no one carries on his skin the spot of idolatry, or fornication, or fraud), so persons of that kind are foul in the spirit, which is the author of the sin; for the spirit is lord, the flesh servant. Yet they each mutually share the guilt: the spirit, on the ground of command; the flesh, of subservience. Therefore, after the waters have been in a manner endued with medicinal virtue[8566] through the intervention of the angel, [8567] the spirit is corporeally washed in the waters, and the flesh is in the same spiritually cleansed.

Chapter V - Use Made of Water by the Heathen. Type of the Angel at the Pool of Bethsaida[8568]

"Well, but the nations, who are strangers to all understanding of spiritual powers, ascribe to their idols the imbuing of waters with the self-same efficacy." (So they do) but they cheat themselves with waters which are widowed. [8569] For washing is the channel through which they are initiated into some sacred rites--of some notorious Isis or Mithras. The gods themselves likewise they honour by washings. Moreover, by carrying water around, and sprinkling it, they everywhere expiate [8570] country-seats, houses, temples, and whole cities: at all events, at the Apollinarian and Eleusinian games they are baptized; and they presume that the effect of their doing that is their regeneration and the remission of the penalties due to their perjuries. Among the ancients, again, whoever had defiled himself with murder, was wont to go in quest of purifying waters. Therefore, if the mere nature of water, in that it is the appropriate material for washing away, leads men to flatter themselves with a belief in omens of purification, how much more truly will waters render that service through the authority of God, by whom all their nature has been constituted! If men think that water is endued with a medicinal virtue by religion, what religion is more effectual than that of the living God?

Which fact being acknowledged, we recognise here also the zeal of the devil rivalling the things of God, [8571] while we find him, too, practising baptism in his subjects. What similarity is there? The unclean cleanses! the ruiner sets free! the damned absolves! He will, forsooth, destroy his own work, by washing away the sins which himself inspires! These (remarks) have been set down by way of testimony against such as reject the faith; if they put no trust in the things of God, the spurious imitations of which, in the case of God's rival, they do trust in. Are there not other cases too, in which, without any sacrament, unclean spirits brood on waters, in spurious imitation of that brooding [8572] of the Divine Spirit in the very beginning?

Witness all shady founts, and all unfrequented brooks, and the ponds in the baths, and the conduits [8573] in private houses, or the cisterns and wells which are said to have the property of "spiriting away," [8574] through the power, that is, of a hurtful spirit. Men whom waters have drowned[8575] or affected with madness or with fear, they call nymph-caught, [8576] or "lymphatic," or "hydro-phobic." Why have we adduced these instances? Lest any think it too hard for belief that a holy angel of God should grant his presence to waters, to temper them to man's salvation; while the evil angel holds frequent profane commerce with the selfsame element to man's ruin. If it seems a novelty for an angel to be present in waters, an example of what was to come to pass has forerun. An angel, by his intervention, was wont to stir the pool at Bethsaida. [8577] They who were complaining of ill-health used to watch for him; for whoever had been the first to descend into them, after his washing, ceased to complain. This figure of corporeal healing sang of a spiritual healing, according to the rule by which things carnal are always antecedent [8578] as figurative of things spiritual. And thus, when the grace of God advanced to higher degrees among men,[8579] an accession of efficacy was granted to the waters and to the angel. They who [8580] were wont to remedy bodily defects, [8581] now heal the spirit; they who used to work temporal salvation [8582] now renew eternal; they who did set free but once in the year, now save peoples in a body[8583] daily, death being done away through ablution of sins. The guilt being removed, of course the penalty is removed too. Thus man will be restored for God to His "likeness," who in days bygone had been conformed to "the image" of God; (the "image" is counted (to be) in his form: the "likeness" in his eternity:) for he receives again that Spirit of God which he had then first received from His afflatus, but had afterward lost through sin.

Chapter VI - The Angel the Forerunner of the Holy Spirit. Meaning Contained in the Baptismal Formula

Not that in [8584] the waters we obtain the Holy Spirit; but in the water, under (the witness of) the angel, we are cleansed, and prepared for the Holy Spirit. In this case also a type has preceded; for thus was John beforehand the Lord's forerunner, "preparing His ways." [8585] Thus, too, does the angel, the witness [8586] of baptism, "make the paths straight" [8587] for the Holy Spirit, who is about to come upon us, by the washing away of sins, which faith, sealed in (the name of) the Father, and the Son, and the Holy Spirit, obtains. For if "in the mouth of three witnesses every word shall stand:" [8588] --while, through the benediction, we have the same (three) as witnesses of our faith whom we have as sureties [8589] of our salvation too--how much more does the number of the divine names suffice for the assurance of our hope likewise!

Moreover, after the pledging both of the attestation of faith and the promise [8590] of salvation under "three witnesses," there is added, of necessity, mention of the Church; [8591] inasmuch as, wherever there are three, (that is, the Father, the Son, and the Holy Spirit,) there is the Church, which is a body of three. [8592]

Chapter VII - Of the Unction

After this, when we have issued from the font, [8593] we are thoroughly anointed with a blessed unction,--(a practice derived) from the old discipline, wherein on entering the priesthood, men were wont to be anointed with oil from a horn, ever since Aaron was anointed by Moses.[8594] Whence Aaron is called "Christ," [8595] from the "chrism," which is "the unction;" which, when made spiritual, furnished an appropriate name to the Lord, because He was "anointed" with the Spirit by God the Father; as written in the Acts: "For truly they were gathered together in this city[8596] against Thy Holy Son whom Thou hast anointed." [8597] Thus, too, in our case, the unction runs carnally, (i.e. on the body,) but profits spiritually; in the same way as the act of baptism itself too is carnal, in that we are plunged in water, but the effect spiritual, in that we are freed from sins.

Chapter VIII - Of the Imposition of Hands. Types of the Deluge and the Dove

In the next place the hand is laid on us, invoking and inviting the Holy Spirit through benediction.[8598] Shall it be granted possible for human ingenuity to summon a spirit into water, and, by the application of hands from above, to animate their union into one body [8599] with another spirit of so clear sound; [8600] and shall it not be possible for God, in the case of His own organ,[8601] to produce, by means of "holy hands," [8602] a sublime spiritual modulation? But this, as well as the former, is derived from the old sacramental rite in which Jacob blessed his grandsons, born of Joseph, Ephrem [8603] and Manasses; with his hands laid on them and interchanged, and indeed so transversely slanted one over the other, that, by delineating Christ, they even portended the future benediction into Christ. [8604] Then, over our cleansed and blessed bodies willingly descends from the Father that Holiest Spirit. Over the waters of baptism, recognising as it were His primeval seat, [8605] He reposes: (He who) glided down on the Lord "in the shape of a dove," [8606] in order that the nature of the Holy Spirit might be declared by means of the creature (the emblem) of simplicity and innocence, because even in her bodily structure the dove is without literal [8607] gall. And accordingly He says, "Be ye simple as doves." [8608] Even this is not without the supporting evidence [8609] of a preceding figure. For just as, after the waters of the deluge, by which the old iniquity was purged-- after the baptism, so to say, of the world--a dove was the herald which announced to the earth the assuagement [8610] of celestial wrath, when she had been sent her way out of the ark, and had returned with the olive-branch, a sign which even among the nations is the fore-token of peace; [8611] so by the self-same law [8612] of heavenly effect, to earth--that is, to our flesh [8613] --as it emerges from the font, [8614] after its old sins flies the dove of the Holy Spirit, bringing us the peace of God, sent out from the heavens where is the Church, the typified ark. [8615] But the world returned unto sin; in which point baptism would ill be compared to the deluge. And so it is destined to fire; just as the man too is, who after baptism renews his sins: [8616] so that this also ought to be accepted as a sign for our admonition.

Chapter IX - Types of the Red Sea, and the Water from the Rock

How many, therefore, are the pleas [8617] of nature, how many the privileges of grace, how many the solemnities of discipline, the figures, the preparations, the prayers, which have ordained the sanctity of water? First, indeed, when the people, set unconditionally free, [8618] escaped the violence of the Egyptian king by crossing over through water, it was water that extinguished [8619] the king himself, with his entire forces. [8620] What figure more manifestly fulfilled in the sacrament of baptism? The nations are set free from the world [8621] by means of water, to wit: and the devil, their old tyrant, they leave quite behind, overwhelmed in the water. Again, water is restored from its defect of "bitterness" to its native grace of "sweetness" by the tree [8622] of Moses. That tree was Christ, [8623] restoring, to wit, of Himself, the veins of sometime envenomed and bitter nature into the all-salutary waters of baptism. This is the water which flowed continuously down for the people from the "accompanying rock;" for if Christ is "the Rock," without doubt we see baptism blest by the water in Christ. How mighty is the grace of water, in the sight of God and His Christ, for the confirmation of baptism!

Never is Christ without water: if, that is, He is Himself baptized in water; [8624] inaugurates in water the first rudimentary displays of His power, when invited to the nuptials; [8625] invites the thirsty, when He makes a discourse, to His own sempiternal water; [8626] approves, when teaching concerning love, [8627] among works of charity, [8628] the cup of water offered to a poor (child);[8629] recruits His strength at a well; [8630] walks over the water; [8631] willingly crosses the sea;[8632] ministers water to His disciples. [8633] Onward even to the passion does the witness of baptism last: while He is being surrendered to the cross, water intervenes; witness Pilate's hands:[8634] when He is wounded, forth from His side bursts water; witness the soldier's lance![8635]

Chapter X - Of John's Baptism

We have spoken, so far as our moderate ability permitted, of the generals which form the groundwork of the sanctity [8636] of baptism. I will now, equally to the best of my power, proceed to the rest of its character, touching certain minor questions.

The baptism announced by John formed the subject, even at that time, of a question, proposed by the Lord Himself indeed to the Pharisees, whether that baptism were heavenly, or truly earthly:[8637] about which they were unable to give a consistent [8638] answer, inasmuch as they understood not, because they believed not. But we, with but as poor a measure of understanding as of faith, are able to determine that that baptism was divine indeed, (yet in respect of the command, not in respect of efficacy [8639] too, in that we read that John was sent by the Lord to perform this duty,)[8640] but human in its nature: for it conveyed nothing celestial, but it fore-ministered to things celestial; being, to wit, appointed over repentance, which is in man's power. [8641] In fact, the doctors of the law and the Pharisees, who were unwilling to "believe," did not "repent" either.[8642] But if repentance is a thing human, its baptism must necessarily be of the same nature:

else, if it had been celestial, it would have given both the Holy Spirit and remission of sins. But none either pardons sins or freely grants the Spirit save God only. [8643] Even the Lord Himself said that the Spirit would not descend on any other condition, but that He should first ascend to the Father. [8644] What the Lord was not yet conferring, of course the servant could not furnish.

Accordingly, in the Acts of the Apostles, we find that men who had "John's baptism" had not received the Holy Spirit, whom they knew not even by hearing. [8645] That, then, was no celestial thing which furnished no celestial (endowments):

whereas the very thing which was celestial in John--the Spirit of prophecy--so completely failed, after the transfer of the whole Spirit to the Lord, that he presently sent to inquire whether He whom he had himself preached, [8646] whom he had pointed out when coming to him, were "HE."[8647] And so "the baptism of repentance" [8648] was dealt with [8649] as if it were a candidate for the remission and sanctification shortly about to follow in Christ: for in that John used to preach "baptism for the remission of sins," [8650] the declaration was made with reference to future remission; if it be true, (as it is,) that repentance is antecedent, remission subsequent; and this is "preparing the way." [8651] But he who "prepares" does not himself "perfect," but procures for another to perfect.

John himself professes that the celestial things are not his, but Christ's, by saying, "He who is from the earth speaketh concerning the earth; He who comes from the realms above is above all;"[8652] and again, by saying that he "baptized in repentance only, but that One would shortly come who would baptize in the Spirit and fire;" [8653] --of course because true and stable faith is baptized with water, unto salvation; pretended and weak faith is baptized with fire, unto judgment.

Chapter XI - Answer to the Objection that "The Lord Did Not Baptize."

"But behold, "say some, "the Lord came, and baptized not; for we read, And yet He used not to baptize, but His disciples!'" [8654] As if, in truth, John had preached that He would baptize with His own hands! Of course, his words are not so to be understood, but as simply spoken after an ordinary manner; just as, for instance, we say, "The emperor set forth an edict," or, "The prefect cudgelled him."

Pray does the emperor in person set forth, or the prefect in person cudgel? One whose ministers do a thing is always said to do it. [8655] So "He will baptize you" will have to be understood as standing for, "Through Him," or "Into Him," "you will be baptized." But let not (the fact) that "He Himself baptized not" trouble any.

For into whom should He baptize? Into repentance? Of what use, then, do you make His forerunner? Into remission of sins, which He used to give by a word? Into Himself, whom by humility He was concealing? Into the Holy Spirit, who had not yet descended from the Father?

Into the Church, which His apostles had not yet founded? And thus it was with the selfsame "baptism of John" that His disciples used to baptize, as ministers, with which John before had baptized as forerunner. Let none think it was with some other, because no other exists, except that of Christ subsequently; which at that time, of course, could not be given by His disciples, inasmuch as the glory of the Lord had not yet been fully attained, [8656] nor the efficacy of the font [8657] established through the passion and the resurrection; because neither can our death see dissolution except by the Lord's passion, nor our life be restored without His resurrection.

Chapter XII - Of the Necessity of Baptism to Salvation

When, however, the prescript is laid down that "without baptism, salvation is attainable by none" (chiefly on the ground of that declaration of the Lord, who says, "Unless one be born of water, he hath not life" [8658]), there arise immediately scrupulous, nay rather audacious, doubts on the part of some, "how, in accordance with that prescript, salvation is attainable by the apostles, whom--Paul excepted--we do not find baptized in the Lord? Nay, since Paul is the only one of them who has put on the garment of Christ's baptism, [8659] either the peril of all the others who lack the water of Christ is prejudged, that the prescript may be maintained, or else the prescript is rescinded if salvation has been ordained even for the unbaptized." I have heard--the Lord is my witness-- doubts of that kind: that none may imagine me so abandoned as to excogitate, unprovoked, in the licence of my pen, ideas which would inspire others with scruple.

And now, as far as I shall be able, I will reply to them who affirm "that the apostles were unbaptized." For if they had undergone the human baptism of John, and were longing for that of the Lord, then since the Lord Himself had defined baptism to be one; [8660] (saying to Peter, who was desirous [8661] of being thoroughly bathed, "He who hath once bathed hath no necessity to wash a second time;" [8662] which, of course, He would not have said at all to one not baptized;) even here we have a conspicuous [8663] proof against those who, in order to destroy the sacrament of water, deprive the apostles even of John's baptism. Can it seem credible that "the way of the Lord," that is, the baptism of John, had not then been "prepared" in those persons who were being destined to open the way of the Lord throughout the whole world? The Lord Himself, though no "repentance" was due from Him, was baptized: was baptism not necessary for sinners?

As for the fact, then, that "others were not baptized"--they, however, were not companions of Christ, but enemies of the faith, doctors of the law and Pharisees. From which fact is gathered an additional suggestion, that, since the opposers of the Lord refused to be baptized, they who followed the Lord were baptized, and were not like-minded with their own rivals: especially when, if there were any one to whom they clave, the Lord had exalted John above him (by the testimony) saying, "Among them who are born of women there is none greater than John the Baptist." [8664]

Others make the suggestion (forced enough, clearly "that the apostles then served the turn of baptism when in their little ship, were sprinkled and covered with the waves: that Peter himself also was immersed enough when he walked on the sea." [8665] It is, however, as I think, one thing to be sprinkled or intercepted by the violence of the sea; another thing to be baptized in obedience to the discipline of religion. But that little ship did present a figure of the Church, in that she is disquieted "in the sea," that is, in the world, [8666] "by the waves," that is, by persecutions and temptations; the Lord, through patience, sleeping as it were, until, roused in their last extremities by the prayers of the saints, He checks the world, [8667] and restores tranquillity to His own.

Now, whether they were baptized in any manner whatever, or whether they continued unbathed [8668] to the end--so that even that saying of the Lord touching the "one bath" [8669] does, under the person of Peter, merely regard us--still, to determine concerning the salvation of the apostles is audacious enough, because on them the prerogative even of first choice, [8670] and thereafter of undivided intimacy, might be able to confer the compendious grace of baptism, seeing they (I think) followed Him who was wont to promise salvation to every believer. "Thy faith," He would say, "hath saved thee;" [8671] and, "Thy sins shall be remitted thee," [8672] on thy believing, of course, albeit thou be not yet baptized. If that [8673] was wanting to the apostles, I know not in the faith of what things it was, that, roused by one word of the Lord, one left the toll-booth behind for ever; [8674] another deserted father and ship, and the craft by which he gained his living;[8675] a third, who disdained his father's obsequies, [8676] fulfilled, before he heard it, that highest precept of the Lord, "He who prefers father or mother to me, is not worthy of me." [8677]

Chapter XIII - Another Objection: Abraham Pleased God Without Being Baptized. Answer Thereto. Old Things Must Give Place to New, and Baptism is Now a Law

Here, then, those miscreants [8678] provoke questions. And so they say, "Baptism is not necessary for them to whom faith is sufficient; for withal, Abraham pleased God by a sacrament of no water, but of faith." But in all cases it is the later things which have a conclusive force, and the subsequent which prevail over the antecedent. Grant that, in days gone by, there was salvation by means of bare faith, before the passion and resurrection of the Lord. But now that faith has been enlarged, and is become a faith which believes in His nativity, passion, and resurrection, there has been an amplification added to the sacrament, [8679] viz., the sealing act of baptism; the clothing, in some sense, of the faith which before was bare, and which cannot exist now without its proper law. For the law of baptizing has been imposed, and the formula prescribed: "Go," He saith, "teach the nations, baptizing them into the name of the Father, and of the Son, and of the Holy Spirit."[8680] The comparison with this law of that definition, "Unless a man have been reborn of water and Spirit, he shall not enter into the kingdom of the heavens," [8681] has tied faith to the necessity of baptism.

Accordingly, all thereafter [8682] who became believers used to be baptized. Then it was, too,[8683] that Paul, when he believed, was baptized; and this is the meaning of the precept which the Lord had given him when smitten with the plague of loss of sight, saying, "Arise, and enter Damascus; there shall be demonstrated to thee what thou oughtest to do," to wit--be baptized, which was the only thing lacking to him. That point excepted, he had sufficiently learnt and believed "the Nazarene" to be "the Lord, the Son of God." [8684]

Chapter XIV - Of Paul's Assertion, that He Had Not Been Sent to Baptize

But they roll back an objection from that apostle himself, in that he said, "For Christ sent me not to baptize;" [8685] as if by this argument baptism were done away!

For if so, why did he baptize Gaius, and Crispus, and the house of Stephanas? [8686] However, even if Christ had not sent him to baptize, yet He had given other apostles the precept to baptize. But these words were written to the Corinthians in regard of the circumstances of that particular time; seeing that schisms and dissensions were agitated among them, while one attributes everything to Paul, another to Apollos. [8687] For which reason the "peace-making" [8688] apostle, for fear he should seem to claim all gifts for himself, says that he had been sent "not to baptize, but to preach." For preaching is the prior thing, baptizing the posterior. Therefore the preaching came first: but I think baptizing withal was lawful to him to whom preaching was.

Chapter XV - Unity of Baptism. Remarks on Heretical And Jewish Baptism

I know not whether any further point is mooted to bring baptism into controversy. Permit me to call to mind what I have omitted above, lest I seem to break off the train of impending thoughts in the middle. There is to us one, and but one, baptism; as well according to the Lord's gospel[8689] as according to the apostle's letters, [8690] inasmuch as he says, "One God, and one baptism, and one church in the heavens." [8691] But it must be admitted that the question, "What rules are to be observed with regard to heretics?" is worthy of being treated. For it is to us [8692] that that assertion[8693] refers. Heretics, however, have no fellowship in our discipline, whom the mere fact of their excommunication [8694] testifies to be outsiders. I am not bound to recognize in them a thing which is enjoined on me, because they and we have not the same God, nor one--that is, the same--Christ. And therefore their baptism is not one with ours either, because it is not the same; a baptism which, since they have it not duly, doubtless they have not at all; nor is that capable of being counted which is not had. [8695] Thus they cannot receive it either, because they have it not. But this point has already received a fuller discussion from us in Greek.

We enter, then, the font [8696] once:

once are sins washed away, because they ought never to be repeated. But the Jewish Israel bathes daily, [8697] because he is daily being defiled: and, for fear that defilement should be practised among us also, therefore was the definition touching the one bathing [8698] made. Happy water, which once washes away; which does not mock sinners (with vain hopes); which does not, by being infected with the repetition of impurities, again defile them whom it has washed!

Chapter XVI - Of the Second Baptism--With Blood

We have indeed, likewise, a second font, [8699] (itself withal one with the former,) of blood, to wit; concerning which the Lord said, "I have to be baptized with a baptism," [8700] when He had been baptized already. For He had come "by means of water and blood," [8701] just as John has written; that He might be baptized by the water, glorified by the blood; to make us, in like manner, called by water, chosen [8702] by blood. These two baptisms He sent out from the wound in His pierced side,[8703] in order that they who believed in His blood might be bathed with the water; they who had been bathed in the water might likewise drink the blood. [8704] This is the baptism which both stands in lieu of the fontal bathing [8705] when that has not been received, and restores it when lost.

Chapter XVII - Of the Power of Conferring Baptism

For concluding our brief subject, [8706] it remains to put you in mind also of the due observance of giving and receiving baptism. Of giving it, the chief priest [8707] (who is the bishop) has the right: in the next place, the presbyters and deacons, yet not without the bishop's authority, on account of the honour of the Church, which being preserved, peace is preserved. Beside these, even laymen have the right; for what is equally received can be equally given. Unless bishops, or priests, or deacons, be on the spot, other disciples are called i.e. to the work. The word of the Lord ought not to be hidden by any: in like manner, too, baptism, which is equally God's property,[8708] can be administered by all. But how much more is the rule [8709] of reverence and modesty incumbent on laymen--seeing that these powers [8710] belong to their superiors--lest they assume to themselves the specific [8711] function of the bishop! Emulation of the episcopal office is the mother of schisms.

The most holy apostle has said, that "all things are lawful, but not all expedient." [8712] Let it suffice assuredly, in cases of necessity, to avail yourself (of that rule [8713], if at any time circumstance either of place, or of time, or of person compels you (so to do); for then the stedfast courage of the succourer, when the situation of the endangered one is urgent, is exceptionally admissible; inasmuch as he will be guilty of a human creature's loss if he shall refrain from bestowing what he had free liberty to bestow. But the woman of pertness, [8714] who has usurped the power to teach, will of course not give birth for herself likewise to a right of baptizing, unless some new beast shall arise [8715] like the former; so that, just as the one abolished baptism, [8716] so some other should in her own right confer it! But if the writings which wrongly go under Paul's name, claim Thecla's example as a licence for women's teaching and baptizing, let them know that, in Asia, the presbyter who composed that writing, [8717] as if he were augmenting Paul's fame from his own store, after being convicted, and confessing that he had done it from love of Paul, was removed[8718] from his office. For how credible would it seem, that he who has not permitted a woman[8719] even to learn with over-boldness, should give a female [8720] the power of teaching and of baptizing! "Let them be silent," he says, "and at home consult their own husbands." [8721]

Chapter XVIII - Of the Persons to Whom, and the Time When, Baptism is to Be Administered

But they whose office it is, know that baptism is not rashly to be administered. "Give to every one who beggeth thee," [8722] has a reference of its own, appertaining especially to almsgiving. On the contrary, this precept is rather to be looked at carefully: "Give not the holy thing to the dogs, nor cast your pearls before swine;" [8723] and, "Lay not hands easily on any; share not other men's sins."[8724] If Philip so "easily" baptized the chamberlain, let us reflect that a manifest and conspicuous [8725] evidence that the Lord deemed him worthy had been interposed. [8726] The Spirit had enjoined Philip to proceed to that road: the eunuch himself, too, was not found idle, nor as one who was suddenly seized with an eager desire to be baptized; but, after going up to the temple for prayer's sake, being intently engaged on the divine Scripture, was thus suitably discovered--to whom God had, unasked, sent an apostle, which one, again, the Spirit bade adjoin himself to the chamberlain's chariot. The Scripture which he was reading [8727] falls in opportunely with his faith: Philip, being requested, is taken to sit beside him; the Lord is pointed out; faith lingers not; water needs no waiting for; the work is completed, and the apostle snatched away.

"But Paul too was, in fact, speedily' baptized:" for Simon, [8728] his host, speedily recognized him to be "an appointed vessel of election." God's approbation sends sure premonitory tokens before it; every "petition" [8729] may both deceive and be deceived. And so, according to the circumstances and disposition, and even age, of each individual, the delay of baptism is preferable; principally, however, in the case of little children. For why is it necessary--if (baptism itself) is not so necessary [8730] --that the sponsors likewise should be thrust into danger? Who both themselves, by reason of mortality, may fail to fulfil their promises, and may be disappointed by the development of an evil disposition, in those for whom they stood? The Lord does indeed say, "Forbid them not to come unto me." [8731] Let them "come," then, while they are growing up; let them "come" while they are learning, while they are learning whither to come; [8732] let them become Christians [8733] when they have become able to know Christ.

Why does the innocent period of life hasten to the "remission of sins?" More caution will be exercised in worldly [8734] matters: so that one who is not trusted with earthly substance is trusted with divine! Let them know how to "ask" for salvation, that you may seem (at least) to have given "to him that asketh." [8735] For no less cause must the unwedded also be deferred--in whom the ground of temptation is prepared, alike in such as never were wedded [8736] by means of their maturity, and in the widowed by means of their freedom--until they either marry, or else be more fully strengthened for continence. If any understand the weighty import of baptism, they will fear its reception more than its delay: sound faith is secure of salvation.

Chapter XIX - Of the Times Most Suitable for Baptism

The Passover affords a more than usually solemn day for baptism; when, withal, the Lord's passion, in which we are baptized, was completed. Nor will it be incongruous to interpret figuratively the fact that, when the Lord was about to celebrate the last Passover, He said to the disciples who were sent to make preparation, "Ye will meet a man bearing water." [8737] He points out the place for celebrating the Passover by the sign of water. After that, Pentecost is a most joyous space [8738] for conferring baptisms; [8739] wherein, too, the resurrection of the Lord was repeatedly proved [8740] among the disciples, and the hope of the advent of the Lord indirectly pointed to, in that, at that time, when He had been received back into the heavens, the angels [8741] told the apostles that "He would so come, as He had withal ascended into the heavens;" [8742] at Pentecost, of course. But, moreover, when Jeremiah says, "And I will gather them together from the extremities of the land in the feast-day," he signifies the day of the Passover and of Pentecost, which is properly a "feast-day." [8743] However, every day is the Lord's; every hour, every time, is apt for baptism: if there is a difference in the solemnity, distinction there is none in the grace.

Chapter XX - Of Preparation For, and Conduct After, the Reception of Baptism

They who are about to enter baptism ought to pray with repeated prayers, fasts, and bendings of the knee, and vigils all the night through, and with the confession of all bygone sins, that they may express the meaning even of the baptism of John: "They were baptized," saith (the Scripture), "confessing their own sins." [8744] To us it is matter for thankfulness if we do now publicly confess our iniquities or our turpitudes: [8745] for we do at the same time both make satisfaction[8746] for our former sins, by mortification of our flesh and spirit, and lay beforehand the foundation of defences against the temptations which will closely follow. "Watch and pray," saith (the Lord), "lest ye fall into temptation." [8747] And the reason, I believe, why they were tempted was, that they fell asleep; so that they deserted the Lord when apprehended, and he who continued to stand by Him, and used the sword, even denied Him thrice: for withal the word had gone before, that "no one untempted should attain the celestial kingdoms." [8748] The Lord Himself forthwith after baptism [8749] temptations surrounded, when in forty days He had kept fast. "Then," some one will say, "it becomes us, too, rather to fast after baptism." [8750] Well, and who forbids you, unless it be the necessity for joy, and the thanksgiving for salvation? But so far as I, with my poor powers, understand, the Lord figuratively retorted upon Israel the reproach they had cast on the Lord.[8751] For the people, after crossing the sea, and being carried about in the desert during forty years, although they were there nourished with divine supplies, nevertheless were more mindful of their belly and their gullet than of God. Thereupon the Lord, driven apart into desert places after baptism, [8752] showed, by maintaining a fast of forty days, that the man of God lives "not by bread alone," but "by the word of God;" [8753] and that temptations incident to fulness or immoderation of appetite are shattered by abstinence. Therefore, blessed ones, whom the grace of God awaits, when you ascend from that most sacred font [8754] of your new birth, and spread your hands[8755] for the first time in the house of your mother, [8756] together with your brethren, ask from the Father, ask from the Lord, that His own specialties of grace and distributions of gifts[8757] may be supplied you. "Ask," saith He, "and ye shall receive." [8758] Well, you have asked, and have received; you have knocked, and it has been opened to you.

Only, I pray that, when you are asking, you be mindful likewise of Tertullian the sinner.[8759]

Elucidation

The argument (p. 673, note 6,) is conclusive, but not clear. The disciples of John must have been baptized by him, (Luke vii. 29-30) and "all the people," must have included those whom Jesus called.

But, this was not Christ's baptism:
See Acts xix. 2, 5. Compare note 8, p. 673. And see the American Editor's "Apollos."

Footnotes:

8542. i.e. Christian (Oehler).

8543. Rationibus.

8544. This curious allusion it is impossible, perhaps, to render in our language. The word IXΘΥΣ (ikhthus) in Greek means "a fish;" and it was used as a name for our Lord Jesus, because the initials of the words Ἰησοῦς Χριστὸς Θεοῦ Υἱὸς Σωτήρ (i.e. Jesus Christ the Son of God, the Savior), make up that word. Oehler with these remarks, gives abundant references on that point. [Dr. Allix suspects Montanism here, but see Kaye, p. 43, and Lardner, Credib. II. p. 335. We may date it circa a.d. 193.]

8545. As being a woman. See 1 Tim. ii. 11, 12.

8546. Consecutio æternitatis.

8547. Admirationem.

8548. i.e. that the simple be vain, and the grand impossible.

8549. 1 Cor. i. 27, not quite exactly quoted.

8550. Luke xviii. 27, again inexact.

8551. Compare the Jews' question, Matt. xxi. 23.

8552. Its authority.

8553. Impolita.

8554. Incomposita.

8555. Ferebatur.

8556. Gen. i. 1, 2, and comp. the LXX.

8557. Liquor.

8558. Gen. i. 6, 7, 8.

8559. Animas.

8560. Animare.

8561. Rebus.

8562. Intinctorum.

8563. Redundat.

8564. Alveo.

8565. Acts viii. 26-40.

8566. Medicatis.

8567. See c. vi. ad init., and c. v. ad fin.

8568. Bethesda, Eng. Ver.

8569. i.e., as Oehler rightly explains, "lacking the Holy Spirit's presence and virtue."

8570. Or, "purify."

8571. [Diabolus Dei Simius.]

8572. Gestationem.

8573. Euripi.

8574. Rapere.

8575. Necaverunt.

8576. "Nympholeptos," restored by Oehler, = νυμφολήπτους.

8577. So Tertullian reads, and some copies, but not the best, of the New Testament in the place referred to, John v. 1-9. [And note Tertullian's textual testimony as to this Scripture.]

8578. Compare 1 Cor. xv. 46.

8579. John i. 16, 17.

8580. Qui: i.e. probably "angeli qui."

8581. Vitia.

8582. Or, "health"--salutem.

8583. Conservant populos.

8584. Compare c. viii., where Tertullian appears to regard the Holy Spirit as given after the baptized had come out of the waters and received the "unction."

8585. Luke i. 76.

8586. Arbiter. [Eccles. v. 6, and Acts xii. 15.]

8587. Isa. xl. 3; Matt. iii. 3.

8588. Deut. xix. 15; Matt. xviii. 16; 2 Cor. xiii. 1.

8589. Sponsores.

8590. Sponsio.

8591. Compare de Orat. c. ii. sub fin.

8592. Compare the de Orat. quoted above, and de Patien. xxi.; and see Matt. xviii. 20.

8593. Lavacro.

8594. See Ex. xxix. 7; Lev. viii. 12; Ps. cxxxiii. 2.

8595. i.e. "Anointed." Aaron, or at least the priest, is actually so called in the LXX., in Lev. iv. 5, 16, ὁ ἱερεὺς ὁ Χριστός: as in the Hebrew it is the word whence Messiah is derived which is used.

8596. Civitate.

8597. Acts iv. 27. "In this city" (ἐν τῇ πόλει ταύτῃ) is omitted in the English version; and the name Ἰησοῦν, "Jesus," is omitted by Tertullian. Compare Acts x. 38 and Lev. iv. 18 with Isa. lxi. 1 in the LXX.

8598. [See Bunsen, Hippol. Vol. III. Sec. xiii. p. 22.]

8599. Concorporationem.

8600. The reference is to certain hydraulic organs, which the editors tell us

are described by Vitruvius, ix. 9 and x. 13, and Pliny, H. N. vii. 37.

8601. i.e. Man. There may be an allusion to Eph. ii. 10, "We are His worksmanship," and to Ps. cl. 4.

8602. Compare 1 Tim. ii. 8.

8603. i.e. Ephraim.

8604. In Christum.

8605. See c. iv. p. 668.

8606. Matt. iii. 16; Luke iii. 22.

8607. Ipso. The ancients held this.

8608. Matt. x. 16. Tertullian has rendered ἀκέραιοι (unmixed) by "simplices," i.e. without fold.

8609. Argumento.

8610. Pacem.

8611. Paci.

8612. Dispositione.

8613. See de Orat. iv. ad init.

8614. Lavacro.

8615. Compare de Idol. xxiv. ad fin.

8616. [2 Pet. i. 9; Heb. x. 26, 27, 29. These awful texts are too little felt by modern Christians. They are too often explained away.]

8617. Patrocinia--"pleas in defence."

8618. "Libere expeditus," set free, and that without any conditions, such as Pharaoh had from time to time tried to impose. See Ex. viii. 25, 28; x. 10, 11, 24.

8619. "Extinxit," as it does fire.

8620. Ex. xiv. 27-30.

8621. Sæculo.

8622. See Ex. xv. 24, 25.

8623. "The Tree of Life," "the True Vine," etc.

8624. Matt. iii. 13-17.

8625. John ii. 1-11.

8626. John vii. 37, 38.

8627. ἀγάπη. See de Orat. c. 28, ad fin.

8628. Dilectionis. See de Patien. c. xii.

8629. Matt. x. 42.

8630. John iv. 6.

8631. Matt. xiv. 25.

8632. Mark iv. 36.

8633. John xiii. 1-12.

8634. Matt. xxvii. 24. Comp. de Orat. c. xiii.

8635. John xix. 34. See c. xviii. sub fin.

8636. Religionem.

8637. Matt. xxi. 25; Mark xi. 30; Luke xx. 4.

8638. Constanter.

8639. Potestate.

8640. See John i. 33.

8641. It is difficult to see how this statement is to be reconciled with Acts v. 31. [i.e. under the universal illumination, John i. 9.]

8642. Matt. iii. 7-12; xxi. 23, 31, 32.

8643. Mark ii. 8; 1 Thess. iv. 8; 2 Cor. i. 21, 22; v. 5.

8644. John xvi. 6, 7.

8645. Acts xix. 1-7. [John vii. 39.]

8646. Matt. iii. 11, 12; John i. 6-36.

8647. Matt. xi. 2-6; Luke vii. 18-23. [He repeats this view.]

8648. Acts xix. 4.

8649. Agebatur.

8650. Mark i. 4.

8651. Luke i. 76.

8652. John iii. 30, 31, briefly quoted.

8653. Matt. iii. 11, not quite exactly given.

8654. John iv. 2.

8655. For instances of this, compare Matt. viii. 5 with Luke vii. 3, 7; and Mark x. 35 with Matt. xx. 20.

8656. Cf. 1 Pet. i. 11, ad fin.

8657. Lavacri.

8658. John iii. 5, not fully given.

8659. See Gal. iii. 27.

8660. See Eph. iv. 5.

8661. "Volenti," which Oehler notes as a suggestion of Fr. Junius, is adopted here in preference to Oehler's "nolenti."

8662. John xiii. 9, 10.

8663. Exerta. Comp. c. xviii. sub init.; ad Ux. ii. c. i. sub fin.

8664. Matt. xi. 11, ἐγήγερται omitted.

8665. Matt. viii. 24; xiv. 28, 29. [Our author seems to allow that sprinkling is baptism, but not Christian baptism: a very curious passage. Compare the foot-washing, John xiii. 8.]

8666. Sæculo.

8667. Sæculum.

8668. Illoti.

8669. Lavacrum. [John xiii. 9, 10, as above.]

8670. i.e. of being the first to be chosen.

8671. Luke xviii. 42; Mark x. 52.

8672. "Remittentur" is Oehler's reading; "remittuntur" others read; but the Greek is in perfect tense. See Mark ii. 5.

8673. i.e. faith, or perhaps the "compendious grace of baptism."

8674. Matt. ix. 9.

8675. Matt. iv. 21, 22.

8676. Luke ix. 59, 60; but it is not said there that the man did it.

8677. Matt. x. 37.

8678. i.e. probably the Cainites. See c. ii.

8679. i.e. the sacrament, or obligation of faith. See beginning of chapter.

8680. Matt. xxviii. 19: "all" omitted.

8681. John ii. 5: "shall not" for "cannot;" "kingdom of the heavens"--an expression only occurring in Matthew--for "kingdom of God."

8682. i.e. from the time when the Lord gave the "law."

8683. i.e. not till after the "law" had been made.

8684. See Acts ix. 1-31.

8685. 1 Cor. i. 17.

8686. 1 Cor. i. 14, 16.

8687. 1 Cor. i. 11, 12; iii. 3, 4.

8688. Matt. v. 9; referred to in de Patien. c. ii.

8689. Oehler refers us to c. xii. above, "He who hath once bathed."

8690. i.e. the Epistle to the Ephesians especially.

8691. Eph. iv. 4, 5, 6, but very inexactly quoted.

8692. i.e. us Christians; of "Catholics," as Oehler explains it.

8693. i.e. touching the "one baptism."

8694. Ademptio communicationis. [See Bunsen, Hippol. III. p. 114, Canon 46.]

8695. Comp. Eccles. i. 15.

8696. Lavacrum.

8697. Compare de Orat. c. xiv.

8698. In John xiii. 10, and Eph. iv. 5.

8699. Lavacrum. [See Aquinas, Quæst. lxvi. 11.]

8700. Luke xii. 50, not given in full.

8701. 1 John v. 6.

8702. Matt. xx. 16; Rev. xvii. 14.

8703. John xix. 34. See c. ix. ad fin.

8704. See John vi. 53, etc.

8705. Lavacrum. [The three baptisms: fluminis, flaminis, sanguinis.]

8706. Materiolam.

8707. Summus sacerdos. Compare de Orat. xxviii., "nos...veri sacerdotes," etc.: and de Ex. Cast. c. vii., "nonne et laici sacerdotes sumus?"

8708. Census.

8709. Disciplina.

8710. i.e. the powers of administering baptism and "sowing the word." [i.e. "The Keys." Scorpiace, p. 643.]

8711. Dicatum.

8712. 1 Cor. x. 23, where μοι in the received text seems interpolated.

8713. Or, as Oehler explains it, of your power of baptizing, etc.

8714. Quintilla. See c. i.

8715. Evenerit. Perhaps Tertullian means literally--though that sense of the word is very rare--"shall issue out of her," alluding to his "pariet" above.

8716. See c. i. ad fin.

8717. The allusion is to a spurious work entitled Acta Pauli et Theclæ. [Of which afterwards. But see Jones, on the Canon, II. p. 353, and Lardner, Credibility, II. p. 305.]

8718. Decessisse.

8719. Mulieri.

8720. Foeminæ.

8721. 1 Cor. xiv. 34, 35.

8722. Luke vi. 30. [See note 4, p. 676.]

8723. Matt. vii. 6.

8724. 1 Tim. v. 22; μηδενὶ omitted, ταχέως rendered by "facile," and μηδὲ by "ne."

8725. "Exertam," as in c. xii.: "probatio exerta," "a conspicuous proof."

8726. Comp. Acts viii. 26-40.

8727. Acts viii. 28, 30, 32, 33, and Isa. liii. 7, 8, especially in LXX. The quotation, as given in Acts, agrees nearly verbatim with the Cod. Alex. there.

8728. Tertullian seems to have confused the "Judas" with whom Saul stayed (Acts ix. 11) with the "Simon" with whom St. Peter stayed (Acts ix. 43); and it was Ananias, not Judas, to whom he was pointed out as "an appointed vessel," and by whom he was baptized. [So above, he seems to have confounded Philip, the deacon, with Philip the apostle.]

8729. See note 24, [where Luke vi. 30 is shown to be abused].

8730. Tertullian has already allowed (in c. xvi) that baptism is not indispensably necessary to salvation.

8731. Matt. xix. 14; Mark x. 14; Luke xviii. 16.

8732. Or, "whither they are coming."

8733. i.e. in baptism.

8734. Sæcularibus.

8735. See beginning of chapter, [where Luke vi. 30, is shown to be abused].

8736. Virginibus; but he is speaking about men as well as women. Comp. de Orat. c. xxii. [I need not point out the bearings of the above chapter, nor do I desire to interpose any comments. The Editor's interpolations, where purely gratuitous, I have even stricken out, though I agree with them. See that work of genius, the Liberty of Prophesying, by Jer. Taylor, sect. xviii. and its candid admissions.]

8737. Mark xiv. 13; Luke xxii. 10, "a small earthen pitcher of water."

8738. [He means the whole fifty days from the Paschal Feast till Pentecost, including the latter. Bunsen Hippol. III. 18.]

8739. Lavacris.

8740. Frequentata, i.e. by His frequent appearance. See Acts i. 3, δι' ἡμερῶν τεσσαράκοντα ὀπτανόμενος αὐτοῖς.

8741. Comp. Acts i. 10 and Luke ix. 30: in each place St. Luke says, ἄνδρες δύο: as also in xxiv. 4 of his Gospel.

8742. Acts i. 10, 11; but it is οὐρανόν throughout in the Greek.

8743. Jer. xxxi. 8, xxxviii. 8 in LXX., where ἐν ἑορτῇ φασέκ is found, which is not in the English version.

8744. Matt. iii. 6. [See the collection of Dr. Bunsen for the whole primitive discipline to which Tertullian has reference, Hippol. Vol. III. pp. 5-23, and 29.]

8745. Perhaps Tertullian is referring to Prov. xxviii. 13. If we confess now, we shall be forgiven, and not put to shame at the judgment day.

8746. See de Orat. c. xxiii. ad fin., and the note there.

8747. Matt. xxvi. 41.

8748. What passage is referred to is doubtful. The editors point us to Luke xxii. 28, 29; but the reference is unsatisfactory.

8749. Lavacrum.

8750. Lavacro. Compare the beginning of the chapter.

8751. Viz. by their murmuring for bread (see Ex. xvi. 3, 7); and again--nearly forty years after--in another place. See Num. xxi. 5.

8752. Aquam: just as St. Paul says the Israelites had been "baptized" (or "baptized themselves") "into Moses in the cloud and in the sea." 1 Cor. x. 2.

8753. Matt. iv. 1-4.

8754. Lavacro.

8755. In prayer: comp. de Orat. c. xiv.

8756. i.e. the Church: comp. de Orat. c. 2.

8757. 1 Cor. xii. 4-12.

8758. Matt. vii. 7; Luke xi. 9; αἰτεῖτε, καὶ δοθήσεται, ὑμῖν in both places.

8759. [The translator, though so learned and helpful, too often encumbers the text with superfluous interpolations. As many of these, while making the reading difficult, add nothing to the sense yet destroy the terse, crabbed force of the original, I have occasionally restored the spirit of a sentence, by removing them.]

III - On Prayer

[Translated by the Rev. S. Thelwall.]

Chapter I - General Introduction [8760]

The Spirit of God, and the Word of God, and the Reason of God--Word of Reason, and Reason and Spirit of Word--Jesus Christ our Lord, namely, who is both the one and the other,[8761] -- has determined for us, the disciples of the New Testament, a new form of prayer; for in this particular also it was needful that new wine should be laid up in new skins, and a new breadth be sewn to a new garment. [8762] Besides, whatever had been in bygone days, has either been quite changed, as circumcision; or else supplemented, as the rest of the Law; or else fulfilled, as Prophecy; or else perfected, as faith itself. For the new grace of God has renewed all things from carnal unto spiritual, by superinducing the Gospel, the obliterator of the whole ancient bygone system; in which our Lord Jesus Christ has been approved as the Spirit of God, and the Word of God, and the Reason of God: the Spirit, by which He was mighty; the Word, by which He taught; the Reason, by which He came. [8763] So the prayer composed by Christ has been composed of three parts. In speech, [8764] by which prayer is enunciated, in spirit, by which alone it prevails, even John had taught his disciples to pray, [8765] but all John's doings were laid as groundwork for Christ, until, when "He had increased"--just as the same John used to fore-announce "that it was needful" that "He should increase and himself decrease" [8766] --the whole work of the forerunner passed over, together with his spirit itself, unto the Lord. Therefore, after what form of words John taught to pray is not extant, because earthly things have given place to heavenly. "He who is from the earth," says John, "speaketh earthly things; and He who is here from the heavens speaketh those things which He hath seen." [8767] And what is the Lord Christ's--as this method of praying is--that is not heavenly? And so, blessed brethren, let us consider His heavenly wisdom: first, touching the precept of praying secretly, whereby He exacted man's faith, that he should be confident that the sight and hearing of Almighty God are present beneath roofs, and extend even into the secret place; and required modesty in faith, that it should offer its religious homage to Him alone, whom it believed to see and to hear everywhere. Further, since wisdom succeeded in the following precept, let it in like manner appertain unto faith, and the modesty of faith, that we think not that the Lord must be approached with a train of words, who, we are certain, takes unsolicited foresight for His own. And yet that very brevity--and let this make for the third grade of wisdom--is supported on the substance of a great and blessed interpretation, and is as diffuse in meaning as it is compressed in words. For it has embraced not only the special duties of prayer, be it veneration of God or petition for man, but almost every discourse of the Lord, every record of His Discipline; so that, in fact, in the Prayer is comprised an epitome of the whole Gospel.

Chapter II - The First Clause

The prayer begins with a testimony to God, and with the reward of faith, when we say, "Our Father who art in the heavens;" for (in so saying), we at once pray to God, and commend faith, whose reward this appellation is.

It is written, "To them who believed on Him He gave power to be called sons of God." [8768] However, our Lord very frequently proclaimed God as a Father to us; nay, even gave a precept "that we call no one on earth father, but the Father whom we have in the heavens:" [8769] and so, in thus praying, we are likewise obeying the precept. Happy they who recognize their Father! This is the reproach that is brought against Israel, to which the Spirit attests heaven and earth, saying, "I have begotten sons, and they have not recognized me." [8770] Moreover, in saying "Father," we also call Him "God." That appellation is one both of filial duty and of power. Again, in the Father the Son is invoked; "for I," saith He, "and the Father are One." [8771] Nor is even our mother the Church passed by, if, that is, in the Father and the Son is recognized the mother, from whom arises the name both of Father and of Son.

In one general term, then, or word, we both honour God, together with His own, [8772] and are mindful of the precept, and set a mark on such as have forgotten their Father.

Chapter III - The Second Clause

The name of "God the Father" had been published to none. Even Moses, who had interrogated Him on that very point, had heard a different name. [8773] To us it has been revealed in the Son, for the Son is now the Father's new name. "I am come," saith He, "in the Father's name;" [8774] and again, "Father, glorify Thy name;" [8775] and more openly, "I have manifested Thy name to men." [8776] That name, therefore, we pray may "be hallowed."

Not that it is becoming for men to wish God well, as if there were any other [8777] by whom He may be wished well, or as if He would suffer unless we do so wish. Plainly, it is universally becoming for God to be blessed [8778] in every place and time, on account of the memory of His benefits ever due from every man. But this petition also serves the turn of a blessing. Otherwise, when is the name of God not "holy," and "hallowed" through Himself, seeing that of Himself He sanctifies all others--He to whom that surrounding circle of angels cease not to say, "Holy, holy, holy?" [8779] In like wise, therefore, we too, candidates for angelhood, if we succeed in deserving it, begin even here on earth to learn by heart that strain hereafter to be raised unto God, and the function of future glory. So far, for the glory of God. On the other hand, for our own petition, when we say, "Hallowed be Thy name," we pray this; that it may be hallowed in us who are in Him, as well in all others for whom the grace of God is still waiting; [8780] that we may obey this precept, too, in "praying for all," [8781] even for our personal enemies. [8782] And therefore with suspended utterance, not saying, "Hallowed be it in us," we say,--"in all."

Chapter IV - The Third Clause

According to this model, [8783] we subjoin, "Thy will be done in the heavens and on the earth;"[8784] not that there is some power withstanding [8785] to prevent God's will being done, and we pray for Him the successful achievement of His will; but we pray for His will to be done in all.

For, by figurative interpretation of flesh and spirit, we are "heaven" and "earth;" albeit, even if it is to be understood simply, still the sense of the petition is the same, that in us God's will be done on earth, to make it possible, namely, for it to be done also in the heavens. What, moreover, does God will, but that we should walk according to His Discipline? We make petition, then, that He supply us with the substance of His will, and the capacity to do it, that we may be saved both in the heavens and on earth; because the sum of His will is the salvation of them whom He has adopted. There is, too, that will of God which the Lord accomplished in preaching, in working, in enduring: for if He Himself proclaimed that He did not His own, but the Father's will, without doubt those things which He used to do were the Father's will; [8786] unto which things, as unto exemplars, we are now provoked; [8787] to preach, to work, to endure even unto death. And we need the will of God, that we may be able to fulfil these duties. Again, in saying, "Thy will be done," we are even wishing well to ourselves, in so far that there is nothing of evil in the will of God; even if, proportionably to each one's deserts, somewhat other [8788] is imposed on us. So by this expression we premonish our own selves unto patience.

The Lord also, when He had wished to demonstrate to us, even in His own flesh, the flesh's infirmity, by the reality of suffering, said, "Father, remove this Thy cup;" and remembering Himself, added, "save that not my will, but Thine be done." [8789] Himself was the Will and the Power of the Father:

and yet, for the demonstration of the patience which was due, He gave Himself up to the Father's Will.

Chapter V - The Fourth Clause

"Thy kingdom come" has also reference to that whereto "Thy will be done" refers--in us, that is. For when does God not reign, in whose hand is the heart of all kings? [8790] But whatever we wish for ourselves we augur for Him, and to Him we attribute what from Him we expect. And so, if the manifestation of the Lord's kingdom pertains unto the will of God and unto our anxious expectation, how do some pray for some protraction of the age, [8791] when the kingdom of God, which we pray may arrive, tends unto the consummation of the age? [8792] Our wish is, that our reign be hastened, not our servitude protracted. Even if it had not been prescribed in the Prayer that we should ask for the advent of the kingdom, we should, unbidden, have sent forth that cry, hastening toward the realization of our hope. The souls of the martyrs beneath the altar [8793] cry in jealousy unto the Lord, "How long, Lord, dost Thou not avenge our blood on the inhabitants of the earth?" [8794] for, of course, their avenging is regulated by [8795] the end of the age. Nay, Lord, Thy kingdom come with all speed,--the prayer of Christians the confusion of the heathen,[8796] the exultation of angels, for the sake of which we suffer, nay, rather, for the sake of which we pray!

Chapter VI - The Fifth Clause

But how gracefully has the Divine Wisdom arranged the order of the prayer; so that after things heavenly--that is, after the "Name" of God, the "Will" of God, and the "Kingdom" of God--it should give earthly necessities also room for a petition! For the Lord had [8797] withal issued His edict, "Seek ye first the kingdom, and then even these shall be added:" [8798] albeit we may rather understand, "Give us this day our daily bread," spiritually. For Christ is our Bread; because Christ is Life, and bread is life. "I am," saith He, "the Bread of Life;" [8799] and, a little above, "The Bread is the Word of the living God, who came down from the heavens." [8800] Then we find, too, that His body is reckoned in bread: "This is my body." [8801] And so, in petitioning for "daily bread," we ask for perpetuity in Christ, and indivisibility from His body. But, because that word is admissible in a carnal sense too, it cannot be so used without the religious remembrance withal of spiritual Discipline; for (the Lord) commands that bread be prayed for, which is the only food necessary for believers; for "all other things the nations seek after." [8802] The like lesson He both inculcates by examples, and repeatedly handles in parables, when He says, "Doth a father take away bread from his children, and hand it to dogs?" [8803] and again, "Doth a father give his son a stone when he asks for bread?" [8804] For He thus shows what it is that sons expect from their father. Nay, even that nocturnal knocker knocked for "bread." [8805] Moreover, He justly added, "Give us this day," seeing He had previously said, "Take no careful thought about the morrow, what ye are to eat." [8806] To which subject He also adapted the parable of the man who pondered on an enlargement of his barns for his forthcoming fruits, and on seasons of prolonged security; but that very night he dies. [8807]

Chapter VII - The Sixth Clause

It was suitable that, after contemplating the liberality of God, [8808] we should likewise address His clemency.

For what will aliments [8809] profit us, if we are really consigned to them, as it were a bull destined for a victim? [8810] The Lord knew Himself to be the only guiltless One, and so He teaches that we beg "to have our debts remitted us." A petition for pardon is a full confession; because he who begs for pardon fully admits his guilt. Thus, too, penitence is demonstrated acceptable to God who desires it rather than the death of the sinner. [8811] Moreover, debt is, in the Scriptures, a figure of guilt; because it is equally due to the sentence of judgment, and is exacted by it: nor does it evade the justice of exaction, unless the exaction be remitted, just as the lord remitted to that slave in the parable his debt; [8812] for hither does the scope of the whole parable tend. For the fact withal, that the same servant, after liberated by his lord, does not equally spare his own debtor; and, being on that account impeached before his lord, is made over to the tormentor to pay the uttermost farthing--that is, every guilt, however small: corresponds with our profession that "we also remit to our debtors;" indeed elsewhere, too, in conformity with this Form of Prayer, He saith, "Remit, and it shall be remitted you." [8813] And when Peter had put the question whether remission were to be granted to a brother seven times, "Nay," saith He, "seventy-seven times;"[8814] in order to remould the Law for the better; because in Genesis vengeance was assigned "seven times" in the case of Cain, but in that of Lamech "seventy-seven times." [8815]

Chapter VIII - The Seventh or Final Clause

For the completeness of so brief a prayer He added--in order that we should supplicate not touching the remitting merely, but touching the entire averting, of acts of guilt--"Lead us not into temptation:" that is, suffer us not to be led into it, by him (of course) who tempts; but far be the thought that the Lord should seem to tempt, [8816] as if He either were ignorant of the faith of any, or else were eager to overthrow it. Infirmity [8817] and malice [8818] are characteristics of the devil. For God had commanded even Abraham to make a sacrifice of his son, for the sake not of tempting, but proving, his faith; in order through him to make an example for that precept of His, whereby He was, by and by, to enjoin that he should hold no pledges of affection dearer than God.[8819] He Himself, when tempted by the devil, demonstrated who it is that presides over and is the originator of temptation. [8820] This passage He confirms by subsequent ones, saying, "Pray that ye be not tempted;" [8821] yet they were tempted, (as they showed) by deserting their Lord, because they had given way rather to sleep than prayer. [8822] The final clause, therefore, is consonant, and interprets the sense of "Lead us not into temptation;" for this sense is, "But convey us away from the Evil One."

Chapter IX - Recapitulation [8823]

In summaries of so few words, how many utterances of the prophets, the Gospels, the apostles--how many discourses, examples, parables of the Lord, are touched on! How many duties are simultaneously discharged! The honour of God in the "Father;" the testimony of faith in the "Name;" the offering of obedience in the "Will;" the commemoration of hope in the "Kingdom;" the petition for life in the "Bread;" the full acknowledgment of debts in the prayer for their "Forgiveness;" the anxious dread of temptation in the request for "Protection." What wonder? God alone could teach how he wished Himself prayed to. The religious rite of prayer therefore, ordained by Himself, and animated, even at the moment when it was issuing out of the Divine mouth, by His own Spirit, ascends, by its own prerogative, into heaven, commending to the Father what the Son has taught.

Chapter X - We May Superadd Prayers of Our Own to the Lord's Prayer

Since, however, the Lord, the Foreseer of human necessities, [8824] said separately, after delivering His Rule of Prayer, "Ask, and ye shall receive;" [8825] and since there are petitions which are made according to the circumstances of each individual; our additional wants have the right-- after beginning with the legitimate and customary prayers as a foundation, as it were--of rearing an outer superstructure of petitions, yet with remembrance of the Master's precepts.

Chapter XI - When Praying the Father, You are Not to Be Angry with a Brother

That we may not be as far from the ears of God as we are from His precepts, [8826] the memory of His precepts paves for our prayers a way unto heaven; of which precepts the chief is, that we go not up unto God's altar [8827] before we compose whatever of discord or offence we have contracted with our brethren. [8828] For what sort of deed is it to approach the peace of God[8829] without peace? the remission of debts [8830] while you retain them? How will he appease his Father who is angry with his brother, when from the beginning "all anger" is forbidden us?[8831] For even Joseph, when dismissing his brethren for the purpose of fetching their father, said, "And be not angry in the way." [8832] He warned us, to be sure, at that time (for elsewhere our Discipline is called "the Way" [8833]), that when, set in "the way" of prayer, we go not unto "the Father" with anger. After that, the Lord, "amplifying the Law," [8834] openly adds the prohibition of anger against a brother to that of murder. [8835] Not even by an evil word does He permit it to be vented. [8836] Ever if we must be angry, our anger must not be maintained beyond sunset, as the apostle admonishes. [8837] But how rash is it either to pass a day without prayer, while you refuse to make satisfaction to your brother; or else, by perseverance in anger, to lose your prayer?

Chapter XII - We Must Be Free Likewise from All Mental Perturbation

Nor merely from anger, but altogether from all perturbation of mind, ought the exercise of prayer to be free, uttered from a spirit such as the Spirit unto whom it is sent. For a defiled spirit cannot be acknowledged by a holy Spirit, [8838] nor a sad by a joyful, [8839] nor a fettered by a free.[8840] No one grants reception to his adversary: no one grants admittance except to his compeer.

Chapter XIII - Of Washing the Hands

But what reason is there in going to prayer with hands indeed washed, but the spirit foul?-- inasmuch as to our hands themselves spiritual purities are necessary, that they may be "lifted up pure"[8841] from falsehood, from murder, from cruelty, from poisonings, [8842] from idolatry, and all the other blemishes which, conceived by the spirit, are effected by the operation of the hands.

These are the true purities; [8843] not those which most are superstitiously careful about, taking water at every prayer, even when they are coming from a bath of the whole body. When I was scrupulously making a thorough investigation of this practice, and searching into the reason of it, I ascertained it to be a commemorative act, bearing on the surrender [8844] of our Lord. We, however, pray to the Lord:

we do not surrender Him; nay, we ought even to set ourselves in opposition to the example of His surrenderer, and not, on that account, wash our hands.

Unless any defilement contracted in human intercourse be a conscientious cause for washing them, they are otherwise clean enough, which together with our whole body we once washed in Christ.[8845]

Chapter XIV - Apostrophe

Albeit Israel washed daily all his limbs over, yet is he never clean. His hands, at all events, are ever unclean, eternally dyed with the blood of the prophets, and of the Lord Himself; and on that account, as being hereditary culprits from their privity to their fathers' crimes, [8846] they do not dare even to raise them unto the Lord, [8847] for fear some Isaiah should cry out, [8848] for fear Christ should utterly shudder.

We, however, not only raise, but even expand them; and, taking our model from the Lord's passion[8849] even in prayer we confess [8850] to Christ.

Chapter XV - Of Putting Off Cloaks

But since we have touched on one special point of empty observance, [8851] it will not be irksome to set our brand likewise on the other points against which the reproach of vanity may deservedly be laid; if, that is, they are observed without the authority of any precept either of the Lord, or else of the apostles. For matters of this kind belong not to religion, but to superstition, being studied, and forced, and of curious rather than rational ceremony; [8852] deserving of restraint, at all events, even on this ground, that they put us on a level with Gentiles. [8853] As, e.g., it is the custom of some to make prayer with cloaks doffed, for so do the nations approach their idols; which practice, of course, were its observance becoming, the apostles, who teach concerning the garb of prayer, [8854] would have comprehended in their instructions, unless any think that is was in prayer that Paul had left his cloak with Carpus! [8855] God, forsooth, would not hear cloaked suppliants, who plainly heard the three saints in the Babylonian king's furnace praying in their trousers and turbans. [8856]

Chapter XVI - Of Sitting After Prayer

Again, for the custom which some have of sitting when prayer is ended, I perceive no reason, except that which children give. [8857] For what if that Hermas, [8858] whose writing is generally inscribed with the title The Shepherd, had, after finishing his prayer, not sat down on his bed, but done some other thing: should we maintain that also as a matter for observance? Of course not. Why, even as it is the sentence, "When I had prayed, and had sat down on my bed," is simply put with a view to the order of the narration, not as a model of discipline.

Else we shall have to pray nowhere except where there is a bed! Nay, whoever sits in a chair or on a bench, will act contrary to that writing. Further: inasmuch as the nations do the like, in sitting down after adoring their petty images; even on this account the practice deserves to be censured in us, because it is observed in the worship of idols. To this is further added the charge of irreverence,--intelligible even to the nations themselves, if they had any sense. If, on the one hand, it is irreverent to sit under the eye, and over against the eye, of him whom you most of all revere and venerate; how much more, on the other hand, is that deed most irreligious under the eye of the living God, while the angel of prayer is still standing by [8859] unless we are upbraiding God that prayer has wearied us!

Chapter XVII - Of Elevated Hands

But we more commend our prayers to God when we pray with modesty and humility, with not even our hands too loftily elevated, but elevated temperately and becomingly; and not even our countenance over-boldly uplifted. For that publican who prayed with humility and dejection not merely in his supplication, but in his countenance too, went his way "more justified" than the shameless Pharisee. [8860] The sounds of our voice, likewise, should be subdued; else, if we are to be heard for our noise, how large windpipes should we need! But God is the hearer not of the voice, but of the heart, just as He is its inspector. The demon of the Pythian oracle says:

"And I do understand the mute, and plainly hear the speechless one." [8861]

Do the ears of God wait for sound? How, then, could Jonah's prayer find way out unto heaven from the depth of the whale's belly, through the entrails of so huge a beast; from the very abysses, through so huge a mass of sea? What superior advantage will they who pray too loudly gain, except that they annoy their neighbours? Nay, by making their petitions audible, what less error do they commit than if they were to pray in public? [8862]

Chapter XVIII - Of the Kiss of Peace

Another custom has now become prevalent. Such as are fasting withhold the kiss of peace, which is the seal of prayer, after prayer made with brethren. But when is peace more to be concluded with brethren than when, at the time of some religious observance, [8863] our prayer ascends with more acceptability; that they may themselves participate in our observance, and thereby be mollified for transacting with their brother touching their own peace? What prayer is complete if divorced from the "holy kiss?" [8864] Whom does peace impede when rendering service to his Lord? What kind of sacrifice is that from which men depart without peace?

Whatever our prayer be, it will not be better than the observance of the precept by which we are bidden to conceal our fasts; [8865] for now, by abstinence from the kiss, we are known to be fasting. But even if there be some reason for this practice, still, lest you offend against this precept, you may perhaps defer your "peace" at home, where it is not possible for your fast to be entirely kept secret. But wherever else you can conceal your observance, you ought to remember the precept:

thus you may satisfy the requirements of Discipline abroad and of custom at home. So, too, on the day of the passover, [8866] when the religious observance of a fast is general, and as it were public, we justly forego the kiss, caring nothing to conceal anything which we do in common with all.

Chapter XIX - Of Stations

Similarly, too, touching the days of Stations, [8867] most think that they must not be present at the sacrificial prayers, on the ground that the Station must be dissolved by reception of the Lord's Body. Does, then, the Eucharist cancel a service devoted to God, or bind it more to God?

Will not your Station be more solemn if you have withal stood at God's altar? [8868] When the Lord's Body has been received and reserved [8869] each point is secured, both the participation of the sacrifice and the discharge of duty. If the "Station" has received its name from the example of military life--for we withal are God's military [8870] --of course no gladness or sadness chanting to the camp abolishes the "stations" of the soldiers: for gladness will carry out discipline more willingly, sadness more carefully.

Chapter XX - Of Women's Dress

So far, however, as regards the dress of women, the variety of observance compels us--men of no consideration whatever--to treat, presumptuously indeed, after the most holy apostle, [8871] except in so far as it will not be presumptuously if we treat the subject in accordance with the apostle. Touching modesty of dress and ornamentation, indeed, the prescription of Peter [8872] likewise is plain, checking as he does with the same mouth, because with the same Spirit, as Paul, the glory of garments, and the pride of gold, and the meretricious elaboration of the hair.

Chapter XXI - Of Virgins

But that point which is promiscuously observed throughout the churches, whether virgins ought to be veiled or no, must be treated of. For they who allow to virgins immunity from head-covering, appear to rest on this; that the apostle has not defined "virgins" by name, but "women," [8873] as "to be veiled;" nor the sex generally, so as to say "females," but a class of the sex, by saying "women:" for if he had named the sex by saying "females," he would have made his limit absolute for every woman; but while he names one class of the sex, he separates another class by being silent. For, they say, he might either have named "virgins" specially; or generally, by a compendious term, "females."

Chapter XXII - Answer to the Foregoing Arguments

They who make this concession [8874] ought to reflect on the nature of the word itself--what is the meaning of "woman" from the very first records of the sacred writings. Here they find it to be the name of the sex, not a class of the sex: if, that is, God gave to Eve, when she had not yet known a man, the surname "woman" and "female" [8875] --("female," whereby the sex generally; "woman," hereby a class of the sex, is marked). [8876] So, since at that time the as yet unwedded Eve was called by the word "woman," that word has been made common even to a virgin. [8877] Nor is it wonderful that the apostle--guided, of course, by the same Spirit by whom, as all the divine Scripture, so that book Genesis, was drawn up--has used the selfsame word in writing "women," which, by the example of Eve unwedded, is applicable too to a "virgin." In fact, all the other passages are in consonance herewith. For even by this very fact, that he has not named "virgins" (as he does in another place [8878] where he is teaching touching marrying), he sufficiently predicates that his remark is made touching every woman, and touching the whole sex; and that there is no distinction made between a "virgin" and any other, while he does not name her at all. For he who elsewhere-- namely, where the difference requires--remembers to make the distinction, (moreover, he makes it by designating each species by their appropriate names,) wishes, where he makes no distinction (while he does not name each), no difference to be understood. What of the fact that in the Greek speech, in which the apostle wrote his letters, it is usual to say, "women" rather than "females;" that is, γυναῖκας (γυναῖκας) rather than θηλείας (θηλείας)? Therefore if that word, [8879] which by interpretation represents what "female" (femina) represents, [8880] is frequently used instead of the name of the sex, [8881] he has named the sex in saying γυναῖκα; but in the sex even the virgin is embraced. But, withal, the declaration is plain: "Every woman," saith he, "praying and prophesying with head uncovered, [8882] dishonoureth her own head." [8883] What is "every woman," but woman of every age, of every rank, of every condition? By saying "every" he excepts nought of womanhood, just as he excepts nought of manhood either from not being covered; for just so he says, "Every man." [8884] As, then, in the masculine sex, under the name of "man" even the "youth" is forbidden to be veiled; so, too, in the feminine, under the name of "woman," even the "virgin" is bidden to be veiled. Equally in each sex let the younger age follow the discipline of the elder; or else let the male "virgins," [8885] too, be veiled, if the female virgins withal are not veiled, because they are not mentioned by name.

Let "man" and "youth" be different, if "woman" and "virgin" are different. For indeed it is "on account of the angels" [8886] that he saith women must be veiled, because on account of "the daughters of men" angels revolted from God. [8887] Who then, would contend that "women" alone-- that is, [8888] such as were already wedded and had lost their virginity--were the objects of angelic concupiscence, unless "virgins" are incapable of excelling in beauty and finding lovers? Nay, let us see whether it were not virgins alone whom they lusted after; since Scriptures saith "the daughters of men;" [8889] inasmuch as it might have named "wives of men," or "females," indifferently. [8890] Likewise, in that it saith, "And they took them to themselves for wives," [8891] it does so on this ground, that, of course, such are "received for wives" as are devoid of that title. But it would have expressed itself differently concerning such as were not thus devoid. And so (they who are named) are devoid as much of widowhood as of virginity. So completely has Paul by naming the sex generally, mingled "daughters" and species together in the genus. Again, while he says that "nature herself," [8892] which has assigned hair as a tegument and ornament to women, "teaches that veiling is the duty of females," has not the same tegument and the same honour of the head been assigned also to virgins?

If "it is shameful" for a woman to be shorn it is similarly so to a virgin too. From them, then, to whom is assigned one and the same law of the head, [8893] one and the same discipline [8894] of the head is exacted,--(which extends) even unto those virgins whom their childhood defends, [8895] for from the first [8896] a virgin was named "female." This custom, [8897] in short, even Israel observes; but if Israel did not observe it, our Law, [8898] amplified and supplemented, would vindicate the addition for itself; let it be excused for imposing the veil on virgins also.

Under our dispensation, let that age which is ignorant of its sex [8899] retain the privilege of simplicity. For both Eve and Adam, when it befell them to be "wise," [8900] forthwith veiled what they had learnt to know. [8901] At all events, with regard to those in whom girlhood has changed (into maturity), their age ought to remember its duties as to nature, so also, to discipline; for they are being transferred to the rank of "women" both in their persons and in their functions. No one is a "virgin" from the time when she is capable of marriage; seeing that, in her, age has by that time been wedded to its own husband, that is, to time. [8902] "But some particular virgin has devoted herself to God. From that very moment she both changes the fashion of her hair, and converts all her garb into that of a woman.'"

Let her, then, maintain the character wholly, and perform the whole function of a "virgin:" what she conceals [8903] for the sake of God, let her cover quite over. [8904] It is our business to entrust to the knowledge of God alone that which the grace of God effects in us, lest we receive from man the reward we hope for from God. [8905] Why do you denude before God [8906] what you cover before men? [8907] Will you be more modest in public than in the church? If your self-devotion is a grace of God, and you have received it, "why do you boast," saith he, "as if you have not received it?" [8908] Why, by your ostentation of yourself, do you judge others? Is it that, by your boasting, you invite others unto good? Nay, but even you yourself run the risk of losing, if you boast; and you drive others unto the same perils! What is assumed from love of boasting is easily destroyed. Be veiled, virgin, if virgin you are; for you ought to blush. If you are a virgin, shrink from (the gaze of) many eyes. Let no one wonder at your face; let no one perceive your falsehood.[8909] You do well in falsely assuming the married character, if you veil your head; nay, you do not seem to assume it falsely, for you are wedded to Christ: to Him you have surrendered your body; act as becomes your Husband's discipline. If He bids the brides of others to be veiled, His own, of course, much more. "But each individual man [8910] is not to think that the institution of his predecessor is to be overturned." Many yield up their own judgment, and its consistency, to the custom of others. Granted that virgins be not compelled to be veiled, at all events such as voluntarily are so should not be prohibited; who, likewise, cannot deny themselves to be virgins,[8911] content, in the security of a good conscience before God, to damage their own fame.[8912] Touching such, however, as are betrothed, I can with constancy "above my small measure"[8913] pronounce and attest that they are to be veiled from that day forth on which they shuddered at the first bodily touch of a man by kiss and hand. For in them everything has been forewedded: their age, through maturity; their flesh, through age; their spirit, through consciousness; their modesty, through the experience of the kiss their hope, through expectation; their mind through volition. And Rebecca is example enough for us, who, when her betrothed had been pointed out, veiled herself for marriage merely on recognition of him. [8914]

Chapter XXIII - Of Kneeling

In the matter of kneeling also prayer is subject to diversity of observance, through the act of some few who abstain from kneeling on the Sabbath; and since this dissension is particularly on its trial before the churches, the Lord will give His grace that the dissentients may either yield, or else indulge their opinion without offence to others. We, however (just as we have received), only on the day of the Lord's Resurrection ought to guard not only against kneeling, but every posture and office of solicitude; deferring even our businesses lest we give any place to the devil. [8915] Similarly, too, in the period of Pentecost; which period we distinguish by the same solemnity of exultation. [8916] But who would hesitate every day to prostrate himself before God, at least in the first prayer with which we enter on the daylight?

At fasts, moreover, and Stations, no prayer should be made without kneeling, and the remaining customary marks of humility; for (then) [8917] we are not only praying, but deprecating, and making satisfaction to God our Lord. [8918] Touching times of prayer nothing at all has been prescribed, except clearly "to pray at every time and every place." [8919]

Chapter XXIV - Of Place for Prayer

But how "in every place," since we are prohibited [8920] (from praying) in public? In every place, he means, which opportunity or even necessity, may have rendered suitable: for that which was done by the apostles [8921] (who, in gaol, in the audience of the prisoners, "began praying and singing to God") is not considered to have been done contrary to the precept; nor yet that which was done by Paul, [8922] who in the ship, in presence of all, "made thanksgiving to God." [8923]

Chapter XXV - Of Time for Prayer

Touching the time, however, the extrinsic [8924] observance of certain hours will not be unprofitable--those common hours, I mean, which mark the intervals of the day--the third, the sixth, the ninth--which we may find in the Scriptures to have been more solemn than the rest. The first infusion of the Holy Spirit into the congregated disciples took place at "the third hour." [8925] Peter, on the day on which he experienced the vision of Universal Community, [8926] (exhibited) in that small vessel, [8927] had ascended into the more lofty parts of the house, for prayer's sake "at the sixth hour." [8928] The same (apostle) was going into the temple, with John, "at the ninth hour," [8929] when he restored the paralytic to his health.

Albeit these practices stand simply without any precept for their observance, still it may be granted a good thing to establish some definite presumption, which may both add stringency to the admonition to pray, and may, as it were by a law, tear us out from our businesses unto such a duty; so that--what we read to have been observed by Daniel also, [8930] in accordance (of course) with Israel's discipline--we pray at least not less than thrice in the day, debtors as we are to Three-- Father, Son, and Holy Spirit: of course, in addition to our regular prayers which are due, without any admonition, on the entrance of light and of night. But, withal, it becomes believers not to take food, and not to go to the bath, before interposing a prayer; for the refreshments and nourishments of the spirit are to be held prior to those of the flesh, and things heavenly prior to things earthly.

Chapter XXVI - Of the Parting of Brethren

You will not dismiss a brother who has entered your house without prayer.--"Have you seen," says Scripture, "a brother? you have seen your Lord;" [8931] --especially "a stranger," lest perhaps he be "an angel."

But again, when received yourself by brethren, you will not make [8932] earthly refreshments prior to heavenly, for your faith will forthwith be judged. Or else how will you--according to the precept[8933] --say, "Peace to this house," unless you exchange mutual peace with them who are in the house?

Chapter XXVII - Of Subjoining a Psalm

The more diligent in prayer are wont to subjoin in their prayers the "Hallelujah," [8934] and such kind of psalms, in the closes of which the company respond. And, of course, every institution is excellent which, for the extolling and honouring of God, aims unitedly to bring Him enriched prayer as a choice victim. [8935]

Chapter XXVIII - Of the Spiritual Victim, Which Prayer is

For this is the spiritual victim [8936] which has abolished the pristine sacrifices.

"To what purpose," saith He, "(bring ye) me the multitude of your sacrifices? I am full of holocausts of rams, and I desire not the fat of rams, and the blood of bulls and of goats. For who hath required these from your hands?" [8937] What, then, God has required the Gospel teaches.

"An hour will come," saith He, "when the true adorers shall adore the Father in spirit and truth. For God is a Spirit, and accordingly requires His adorers to be such." [8938] We are the true adorers and the true priests, [8939] who, praying in spirit, [8940] sacrifice, in spirit, prayer,--a victim proper and acceptable to God, which assuredly He has required, which He has looked forward to [8941] for Himself! This victim, devoted from the whole heart, fed on faith, tended by truth, entire in innocence, pure in chastity, garlanded with love, [8942] we ought to escort with the pomp[8943] of good works, amid psalms and hymns, unto God's altar, [8944] to obtain for us all things from God.

Chapter XXIX - Of the Power of Prayer

For what has God, who exacts it ever denied [8945] to prayer coming from "spirit and truth?"

How mighty specimens of its efficacy do we read, and hear, and believe! Old-world prayer, indeed, used to free from fires, [8946] and from beasts, [8947] and from famine; [8948] and yet it had not (then) received its form from Christ. But how far more amply operative is Christian prayer! It does not station the angel of dew in mid-fires, [8949] nor muzzle lions, nor transfer to the hungry the rustics' bread; [8950] it has no delegated grace to avert any sense of suffering; [8951] but it supplies the suffering, and the feeling, and the grieving, with endurance: it amplifies grace by virtue, that faith may know what she obtains from the Lord, understanding what--for God's name's sake--she suffers. But in days gone by, withal prayer used to call down [8952] plagues, scatter the armies of foes, withhold the wholesome influences of the showers. Now, however, the prayer of righteousness averts all God's anger, keeps bivouac on behalf of personal enemies, makes supplication on behalf of persecutors. Is it wonder if it knows how to extort the rains of heaven[8953] --(prayer) which was once able to procure its fires? [8954] Prayer is alone that which vanquishes[8955] God. But Christ has willed that it be operative for no evil: He had conferred on it all its virtue in the cause of good.

And so it knows nothing save how to recall the souls of the departed from the very path of death, to transform the weak, to restore the sick, to purge the possessed, to open prison-bars, to loose the bonds of the innocent. Likewise it washes away faults, repels temptations, extinguishes persecutions, consoles the faint-spirited, cheers the high-spirited, escorts travellers, appeases waves, makes robbers stand aghast, nourishes the poor, governs the rich, upraises the fallen, arrests the falling, confirms the standing. Prayer is the wall of faith: her arms and missiles [8956] against the foe who keeps watch over us on all sides. And, so never walk we unarmed. By day, be we mindful of Station; by night, of vigil. Under the arms of prayer guard we the standard of our General; await we in prayer the angel's trump. [8957] The angels, likewise, all pray; every creature prays; cattle and wild beasts pray and bend their knees; and when they issue from their layers and lairs, [8958] they look up heavenward with no idle mouth, making their breath vibrate [8959] after their own manner. Nay, the birds too, rising out of the nest, upraise themselves heavenward, and, instead of hands, expand the cross of their wings, and say somewhat to seem like prayer. [8960] What more then, touching the office of prayer? Even the Lord Himself prayed; to whom be honour and virtue unto the ages of the ages!

Footnotes:

8760. [After the discipline of Repentance and of Baptism the Laws of Christian Living come into view. Hence this is the logical place for this treatise. See the Prolegomena of Muratori and learned annotations, in Routh, Opuscula I. p. 173, et sqq. We may date it circa a.d. 192. For much of the Primitive Discipline, concerning Prayer, see Bunsen, Hippol. III. pp. 88-91, etc.]

8761. Oehler's punctuation is followed here. The sentence is difficult, and has perplexed editors and commentators considerably.

8762. Matt. ix. 16, 17; Mark ii. 21, 22; Luke v. 36, 37.

8763. Routh suggests, "fortase quâ sensit," referring to the Adv. Praxeam, c. 5.

8764. Sermone.

8765. This is Oehler's punctuation. The edition of Pamelius reads: "So the prayer composed by Christ was composed of three parts: of the speech, by which it is enunciated; of the spirit, by which alone it prevails; of the reason, by which it is taught."

Rigaltius and subsequent editors read, "of the reason, by which it is conceived;" but this last clause is lacking in the mss., and Oehler's reading appears, as he says, to "have healed the words." [Oehler's punctuation must stand; but, the preceding sentence justifies the interpolation of Rigaltius and heals more effectually.]

8766. John iii. 30.

8767. John iii. 31, 32.

8768. John i. 12.

8769. Matt. xxiii. 9.

8770. Isa. i. 2.

8771. John x. 30.

8772. "i.e., together with the Son and the Holy Spirit" (Oehler); "His Son and His church" (Dodgson).

8773. Ex. iii. 13-16.

8774. John v. 43.

8775. John xii. 28.

8776. John xvii. 6.

8777. i.e., "any other god."

8778. Ps. ciii. 22.

8779. Isa. vi. 3; Rev. iv. 8.

8780. Isa. xxx. 18.

8781. 1 Tim. ii. 1.

8782. Matt. v. 44.

8783. Mr. Dodgson renders, "next to this clause;" but the "forma" referred to seems, by what Tertullian proceeds to add, to be what he had said above, "not that it becomes us to wish God well," etc.

8784. We learn from this and other places, that the comparative adverb was wanting in some ancient formulæ of the Lord's Prayer. [See Routh, Opuscula I. p. 178.]

8785. See note 3.

8786. John vi. 38.

8787. For this use of the word "provoke," see Heb. x. 24, Eng. ver.

8788. [Something we might think other than good.]

8789. Luke xxii. 42.

8790. Prov. xxi. 1.

8791. Or, "world," sæculo.

8792. Or, "world," sæculi. See Matt. xxiv. 3, especially in the Greek. By "praying for some protraction in the age," Tertullian appears to refer to some who used to pray that the end might be deferred (Rigalt.).

8793. altari.

8794. Rev. vi. 10.

8795. So Dodgson aptly renders "dirigitur a."

8796. [See Ad Nationes, p. 128, supra.]

8797. This is a slight mistake of Tertullian. The words referred to, "Seek ye first," etc., do not occur till the end of the chapter in which the prayer is found, so that his pluperfect is out of place. [He must have been aware of this: he only gives logical order to the thought which existed in the divine mind. See note 10, p. 682.]

8798. Matt. vi. 33.

8799. John vi. 35.

8800. John vi. 33.

8801. Matt. xxvi. 26.

8802. Matt. vi. 32.

8803. Tertullian seems to refer to Matt. xv. 26; Mark vii. 27.

8804. Matt. vii. 9; Luke xi. 11.

8805. Luke xi. 5-9.

8806. Matt. vi. 34 and Luke xii. 29 seem to be referred to; but the same remark applies as in note 10 on the preceding page.

8807. Luke xii. 16-20.

8808. In the former petition, "Give us this day our daily bread."

8809. Such as "daily bread."

8810. That is, if we are just to be fed and fattened by them in body, as a bull which is destined for sacrifice is, and then, like him, slain--handed over to death?

8811. Ex. xviii. 23, 32; xxxiii. 11.

8812. Matt. xviii. 21-35.

8813. Luke vi. 37.

8814. Matt. xviii. 21-22.

8815. Gen. iv. 15, 24.

8816. See James i. 13.

8817. Implied in the one hypothesis--ignorance.

8818. Implied in the other--wishing to overthrow faith.

8819. i.e. no children even. The reference is apparently to Matt. x. 37 and Luke xiv. 26, with which may be compared Deut. xiii. 6-10 and xxxiii. 9. If Oehler's reading, which I have followed, be correct, the precept, which is not verbally given till ages after Abraham, is made to have a retrospective force on him.

8820. See Matt. iv. 10; Luke iv. 8.

8821. Luke xxii. 40; Matt. xxvi. 41; Mark xiv. 31.

8822. Routh refers us to De Bapt. c. 20, where Tertullian refers to the same event. [Note also his reference to De Fuga, cap. ii.]

8823. Here comes in the Codex Ambrosianus, with the title, "Here begins a treatise of Tertullian of divers necessary things;" and from it are taken the headings of the remaining chapters. (See Oehler and Routh.)

8824. See Matt. vi. 8.

8825. Matt. vii. 7; Luke xi. 9.

8826. Oehler divides these two chapters as above. The generally adopted division unites this sentence to the preceding chapter, and begins the new chapter with, "The memory of His precepts;" and perhaps this is the preferable division.

8827. altare. [Heb. xiii. 10.]

8828. Matt. v. 22, 23.

8829. Perhaps there may be an allusion to Phil. iv. 6, 7.

8830. See chap. vii. above, and compare Matt. vi. 14, 15.

8831. "Ab initio" probably refers to the book of Genesis, the initium, or beginning of Scripture, to which he is about to refer. But see likewise Eph. iv. 31, Matt. v. 21, 22. [Gen. iv. 6, 7.]

8832. Gen. xlv. 24: so the LXX.

8833. See Acts ix. 2; xix. 9, 23, in the Greek.

8834. See Matt. v. 17.

8835. Matt. v. 21, 22.

8836. Matt. v. 21, 22; 1 Pet. iii. 9, etc.

8837. Eph. iv. 26.

8838. Eph. iv. 30.

8839. John xvii. 14; Rom. xiv. 17.

8840. Ps. li. 12.

8841. 1 Tim. ii. 8.

8842. Or, "sorceries."

8843. See Matt. xv. 10, 11, 17-20; xxiii. 25, 26.

8844. By Pilate. See Matt. xxvii. 24. [N. B. quoad Ritualia.]

8845. i.e. in baptism.

8846. See Matt. xxiii. 31; Luke xi. 48.

8847. I do not know Tertullian's authority for this statement. Certainly Solomon did raise his hands (1 Kings viii. 54), and David apparently his (see Ps. cxliii. 6; xxviii. 2; lxii. 4, etc.). Compare, too, Ex. xvii. 11, 12. But probably he is speaking only of the Israel of his own day. [Evidently.]

8848. Isa. i. 15.

8849. i.e. from the expansion of the hands on the cross.

8850. Or, "give praise."

8851. i.e. the hand-washing.

8852. Or, "reasonable service." See Rom. xii. 1.

8853. Or, "Gentile practices."

8854. See 1 Cor. xi. 3-16.

8855. 2 Tim. iv. 13.

8856. Dan. iii. 21, etc.

8857. i.e. that they have seen it done; for children imitate anything and everything (Oehler).

8858. [Vol. II. p. 18 (Vision V.), this Series. Also, Ib. p. 57, note 2. See Routh's quotation from Cotelerius, p. 180, in Volume before noted.]

8859. Routh and Oehler (after Rigaltius) refer us to Tob. xii. 12. They also, with Dodgson, refer to Luke i. 11. Perhaps there may be a reference to Rev. viii. 3, 4.

8860. Luke xviii. 9-14.

8861. Herod. i. 47.

8862. Which is forbidden, Matt. vi. 5, 6.

8863. Such as fasting.

8864. See Rom. xvi. 16; 1 Cor. xvi. 20; 2 Cor. xiii. 12; 1 Thess. v. 26; 1 Pet. v. 14. [The sexes apart.]

8865. Matt. vi. 16-18.

8866. i.e. "Good Friday," as it is now generally called.

8867. The word Statio seems to have been used in more than one sense in the ancient Church. A passage in the Shepherd of Hermas, referred to above (B. iii. Sim. 5), appears to make it ="fast."

8868. "Ara," not "altare."

8869. For receiving at home apparently, when your station is over.

8870. See 2 Tim. ii. 1, etc. [See Hermas, Vol. I., p. 33.]

8871. See 1 Cor. xi. 1-16; 1 Tim. ii. 9, 10.

8872. 1 Pet. iii. 1-6.

8873. 1 Cor. xi. 5.

8874. As to the distinction between "women" and "virgins."

8875. Gen. ii. 23. In the LXX. and in the Eng. ver. there is but the one word "woman."

8876. These words are regarded by Dr. Routh as spurious, and not without reason. Mr. Dodgson likewise omits them, and refers to de Virg. Vel. cc. 4 and 5.

8877. In de Virg. Vel. 5, Tertullian speaks even more strongly: "And so you have the name, I say not now common, but proper to a virgin; a name which from the beginning a virgin received."

8878. 1 Cor. vii. 34 et seq.

8879. γυνή.

8880. Mr. Dodgson appears to think that there is some transposition here; and at first sight it may appear so. But when we look more closely, perhaps there is no need to make any difficulty: the stress is rather on the words "by interpretation," which, of course, is a different thing from "usage;" and by interpretation γυνή appears to come nearer to "femina" than to "mulier."

8881. θηλεῖα.

8882. Or, "unveiled."

8883. 1 Cor. xi. 5.

8884. 1 Cor. xi. 4.

8885. For a similar use of the word "virgin," see Rev. xiv. 4.

8886. 1 Cor. xi. 10.

8887. See Gen. vi. 2 in the LXX., with the v. l. ed. Tisch. 1860; and compare Tertullian, de Idol. c. 9, and the note there. Mr. Dodgson refers, too, to de Virg. Vel. c. 7, where this curious subject is more fully entered into.

8888. i.e. according to their definition, whom Tertullian is refuting.

8889. Gen. iv. 2.

8890. i.e. If married women had been meant, either word, "uxores" or "feminæ," could have been used indifferently.

8891. Gen. vi. 2.

8892. 1 Cor. xi. 14.

8893. i.e. long hair.

8894. i.e. veiling.

8895. i.e. "exempts."

8896. i.e. from her creation.

8897. Of the "universal veiling of women."

8898. i.e. as above, the Sermon on the Mount.

8899. i.e. mere infancy.

8900. Gen. iii. 6.

8901. Gen. ii. 27 (or in the LXX. iii. 1), and iii. 7, 10, 11.

8902. Routh refers us to de Virg. Vel. c. 11.

8903. i.e. the redundance of her hair.

8904. i.e. by a veil.

8905. i.e. says Oehler, "lest we postpone the eternal favour of God, which we hope for, to the temporal veneration of men; a risk which those virgins seemed likely to run who, when devoted to God, used to go veiled in public, but bareheaded in the church."

8906. i.e. in church.

8907. i.e. in public; see note 27, supra.

8908. 1 Cor. iv. 7.

8909. i.e. as Muratori, quoted by Oehler, says, your "pious" (?) fraud in pretending to be married when you are a virgin; because "devoted" virgins used to dress and wear veils like married women, as being regarded as "wedded to Christ."

8910. i.e. each president of a church, or bishop.

8911. i.e. "are known to be such through the chastity of their manner and life" (Oehler).

8912. "By appearing in public as married women, while in heart they are virgins" (Oehler).

8913. Does Tertullian refer to 2 Cor. x. 13? or does "modulus" mean, as Oehler thinks, "my rule?" [It seems to me a very plain reference to the text before mentioned, and to the Apostolic Canon of not exceeding one's Mission.]

8914. Gen. xxiv. 64, 65.

8915. Eph. iv. 27.

8916. i.e. abstaining from kneeling: kneeling being more "a posture of solicitude" and of humility; standing, of "exultation."

8917. i.e. at fasts and Stations. [Sabbath = Saturday, supra.]

8918. For the meaning of "satisfaction" as used by the Fathers, see Hooker, Eccl. Pol. vi. 5.

8919. Eph. vi. 18; 1 Thess. v. 17; 1 Tim. ii. 8.

8920. Matt. vi. 5, 6, which forbids praying in public.

8921. Paul and Silas (Acts xvi. 25).

8922. I have followed Muratori's reading here.

8923. Mr. Dodgson renders "celebrated the Eucharist;" but that rendering appears very doubtful. See Acts xxvii. 35.

8924. Mr. Dodgson supposes this word to mean "outward, as contrasted with the inward, praying always.'" Oehler interprets, "ex vita communi." But perhaps what Tertullian says lower down in the chapter, "albeit they stand simply without any precept enjoining their observance," may give us the true clue to his meaning; so that "extrinsecus" would ="extrinsic to any direct injunction of our Lord or His apostles."

8925. Acts ii. 1-4, 14, 15.

8926. Communitatis omnis (Oehler). Mr. Dodgson renders, "of every sort of common thing." Perhaps, as Routh suggests, we should read "omnium."

8927. Vasculo. But in Acts it is, σκεῦός τι ὡς ὀθόνην μεγάλην [Small is here comparatively used, with reference to Universality of which it was the symbol.]

8928. Acts x. 9.

8929. Acts iii. 1: but the man is not said to have been "paralytic," but "lame from his mother's womb."

8930. Dan. vi. 10; comp. Ps. lv. 17 (in the LXX. it is liv. 18).

8931. I have ventured to turn the first part of the sentence into a question. What "scripture" this may be, no one knows. [It seems to me a clear reference to Matt. xxv. 38, amplified by the 45th verse, in a way not unusual with our author.] Perhaps, in addition to the passages in Gen. xviii. and Heb. xiii. 2, to which the editors naturally refer, Tertullian may allude to such passages as Mark. ix. 37; Matt. xxv. 40, 45. [Christo in pauperibus.]

8932. I have followed Routh's conjecture, "feceris" for "fecerit," which Oehler does not even notice.

8933. Luke x. 5.

8934. Perhaps "the great Hallelujah," i.e. the last five psalms.

8935. [The author seems to have in mind (Hos. xiv. 2) "the calves of our lips."]

8936. 1 Pet. ii. 5.

8937. Isa. i. 11. See the LXX.

8938. John iv. 23, 24.

8939. Sacerdotes; comp. de Ex. Cast. c. 7.

8940. 1 Cor. xiv. 15; Eph. vi. 18.

8941. Or, "provided."

8942. "ἀγάπη," perhaps "the love-feast."

8943. Or, "procession."

8944. Altare.

8945. Routh would read, "What will God deny?"

8946. Dan. iii.

8947. Dan. vi.

8948. 1 Kings xviii.; James v. 17, 18.

8949. i.e. "the angel who preserved in the furnace the three youths besprinkled, as it were, with dewy shower" (Muratori quoted by Oehler).

[Apocrypha, The Song, etc., verses 26, 27.]

8950. 2 Kings iv. 42-44.

8951. i.e. in brief, its miraculous operations, as they are called, are suspended in these ways.

8952. Or, "inflict."

8953. See Apolog. c. 5 (Oehler).

8954. See 2 Kings i.

8955. [A reference to Jacob's wrestling. Also, probably, to Matt. xi. 12.]

8956. Or, "her armour defensive and offensive."

8957. 1 Cor. xv. 52; 1 Thess. iv. 16.

8958. Or, "pens and dens."

8959. As if in prayer.

8960. This beautiful passage should be supplemented by a similar one from St. Bernard: "Nonne et aviculas levat, non onerat pennarum numerositas ipsa? Tolle eas, et reliquum corpus pondere suo fertur ad ima. Sic disciplinam Christi, sic suave jugum, sic onus leve, quo deponimus, eo deprimimur ipsi:

quia portat potius quam portatur." Epistola, ccclxxxv. Bernardi Opp. Tom. i. p. 691. Ed. (Mabillon.) Gaume, Paris, 1839. Bearing the cross uplifts the Christian.]

IV - Ad Martyras *8961*

[Translated by the Rev. S. Thelwall.]

Chapter I

Blessed Martyrs Designate,--Along with the provision which our lady mother the Church from her bountiful breasts, and each brother out of his private means, makes for your bodily wants in the prison, accept also from me some contribution to your spiritual sustenance; for it is not good that the flesh be feasted and the spirit starve: nay, if that which is weak be carefully looked to, it is but right that that which is still weaker should not be neglected. Not that I am specially entitled to exhort you; yet not only the trainers and overseers, but even the unskilled, nay, all who choose, without the slightest need for it, are wont to animate from afar by their cries the most accomplished gladiators, and from the mere throng of onlookers useful suggestions have sometimes come; first, then, O blessed, grieve not the Holy Spirit, [8962] who has entered the prison with you; for if He had not gone with you there, you would not have been there this day. Do you give all endeavour, therefore, to retain Him; so let Him lead you thence to your Lord. The prison, indeed, is the devil's house as well, wherein he keeps his family. But you have come within its walls for the very purpose of trampling the wicked one under foot in his chosen abode. You had already in pitched battle outside utterly overcome him; let him have no reason, then, to say to himself, "They are now in my domain; with vile hatreds I shall tempt them, with defections or dissensions among themselves." Let him fly from your presence, and skulk away into his own abysses, shrunken and torpid, as though he were an outcharmed or smoked-out snake. Give him not the success in his own kingdom of setting you at variance with each other, but let him find you armed and fortified with concord; for peace among you is battle with him. Some, not able to find this peace in the Church, have been used to seek it from the imprisoned martyrs. [8963] And so you ought to have it dwelling with you, and to cherish it, and to guard it, that you may be able perhaps to bestow it upon others.

Chapter II

Other things, hindrances equally of the soul, may have accompanied you as far as the prison gate, to which also your relatives may have attended you. There and thenceforth you were severed from the world; how much more from the ordinary course of worldly life and all its affairs! Nor let this separation from the world alarm you; for if we reflect that the world is more really the prison, we shall see that you have gone out of a prison rather than into one. The world has the greater darkness, blinding men's hearts. The world imposes the more grievous fetters, binding men's very souls.

The world breathes out the worst impurities--human lusts. The world contains the larger number of criminals, even the whole human race.

Then, last of all, it awaits the judgment, not of the proconsul, but of God. Wherefore, O blessed, you may regard yourselves as having been translated from a prison to, we may say, a place of safety. It is full of darkness, but ye yourselves are light; it has bonds, but God has made you free. Unpleasant exhalations are there, but ye are an odour of sweetness. The judge is daily looked for, but ye shall judge the judges themselves.

Sadness may be there for him who sighs for the world's enjoyments. The Christian outside the prison has renounced the world, but in the prison he has renounced a prison too. It is of no consequence where you are in the world--you who are not of it. And if you have lost some of life's sweets, it is the way of business to suffer present loss, that after gains may be the larger.

Thus far I say nothing of the rewards to which God invites the martyrs. Meanwhile let us compare the life of the world and of the prison, and see if the spirit does not gain more in the prison than the flesh loses. Nay, by the care of the Church and the love of the brethren, [8964] even the flesh does not lose there what is for its good, while the spirit obtains besides important advantages. You have no occasion to look on strange gods, you do not run against their images; you have no part in heathen holidays, even by mere bodily mingling in them; you are not annoyed by the foul fumes of idolatrous solemnities; you are not pained by the noise of the public shows, nor by the atrocity or madness or immodesty of their celebrants; your eyes do not fall on stews and brothels; you are free from causes of offence, from temptations, from unholy reminiscences; you are free now from persecution too. The prison does the same service for the Christian which the desert did for the prophet.

Our Lord Himself spent much of His time in seclusion, that He might have greater liberty to pray, that He might be quit of the world. It was in a mountain solitude, too, He showed His glory to the disciples. Let us drop the name of prison; let us call it a place of retirement. Though the body is shut in, though the flesh is confined, all things are open to the spirit.

In spirit, then, roam abroad; in spirit walk about, not setting before you shady paths or long colonnades, but the way which leads to God. As often as in spirit your footsteps are there, so often you will not be in bonds. The leg does not feel the chain when the mind is in the heavens. The mind compasses the whole man about, and whither it wills it carries him. But where thy heart shall be, there shall be thy treasure. [8965] Be there our heart, then, where we would have our treasure.

Chapter III

Grant now, O blessed, that even to Christians the prison is unpleasant; yet we were called to the warfare of the living God in our very response to the sacramental words. Well, no soldier comes out to the campaign laden with luxuries, nor does he go to action from his comfortable chamber, but from the light and narrow tent, where every kind of hardness, roughness and unpleasantness must be put up with. Even in peace soldiers inure themselves to war by toils and inconveniences-- marching in arms, running over the plain, working at the ditch, making the testudo, engaging in many arduous labours. The sweat of the brow is on everything, that bodies and minds may not shrink at having to pass from shade to sunshine, from sunshine to icy cold, from the robe of peace to the coat of mail, from silence to clamour, from quiet to tumult. In like manner, O blessed ones, count whatever is hard in this lot of yours as a discipline of your powers of mind and body.

You are about to pass through a noble struggle, in which the living God acts the part of superintendent, in which the Holy Ghost is your trainer, in which the prize is an eternal crown of angelic essence, citizenship in the heavens, glory everlasting. Therefore your Master, Jesus Christ, who has anointed you with His Spirit, and led you forth to the arena, has seen it good, before the day of conflict, to take you from a condition more pleasant in itself, and has imposed on you a harder treatment, that your strength might be the greater. For the athletes, too, are set apart to a more stringent discipline, that they may have their physical powers built up. They are kept from luxury, from daintier meats, from more pleasant drinks; they are pressed, racked, worn out; the harder their labours in the preparatory training, the stronger is the hope of victory. "And they," says the apostle, "that they may obtain a corruptible crown." [8966] We, with the crown eternal in our eye, look upon the prison as our training-ground, that at the goal of final judgment we may be brought forth well disciplined by many a trial; since virtue is built up by hardships, as by voluptuous indulgence it is overthrown.

Chapter IV

From the saying of our Lord we know that the flesh is weak, the spirit willing. [8967] Let us not, withal, take delusive comfort from the Lord's acknowledgment of the weakness of the flesh. For precisely on this account He first declared the spirit willing, that He might show which of the two ought to be subject to the other--that the flesh might yield obedience to the spirit--the weaker to the stronger; the former thus from the latter getting strength. Let the spirit hold convene with the flesh about the common salvation, thinking no longer of the troubles of the prison, but of the wrestle and conflict for which they are the preparation. The flesh, perhaps, will dread the merciless sword, and the lofty cross, and the rage of the wild beasts, and that punishment of the flames, of all most terrible, and all the skill of the executioner in torture. But, on the other side, let the spirit set clearly before both itself and the flesh, how these things, though exceeding painful, have yet been calmly endured by many,--and, have even been eagerly desired for the sake of fame and glory; and this not only in the case of men, but of women too, that you, O holy women, may be worthy of your sex. It would take me too long to enumerate one by one the men who at their own self-impulse have put an end to themselves. As to women, there is a famous case at hand: the violated Lucretia, in the presence of her kinsfolk, plunged the knife into herself, that she might have glory for her chastity.

Mucius burned his right hand on an altar, that this deed of his might dwell in fame. The philosophers have been outstripped,--for instance Heraclitus, who, smeared with cow dung, burned himself; and Empedocles, who leapt down into the fires of Ætna; and Peregrinus, [8968] who not long ago threw himself on the funeral pile. For women even have despised the flames. Dido did so, lest, after the death of a husband very dear to her, she should be compelled to marry again; and so did the wife of Hasdrubal, who, Carthage being on fire, that she might not behold her husband suppliant as Scipio's feet, rushed with her children into the conflagration, in which her native city was destroyed. Regulus, a Roman general, who had been taken prisoner by the Carthaginians, declined to be exchanged for a large number of Carthaginian captives, choosing rather to be given back to the enemy. He was crammed into a sort of chest; and, everywhere pierced by nails driven from the outside, he endured so many crucifixions. Woman has voluntarily sought the wild beasts, and even asps, those serpents worse than bear or bull, which Cleopatra applied to herself, that she might not fall into the hands of her enemy. But the fear of death is not so great as the fear of torture. And so the Athenian courtezan succumbed to the executioner, when, subjected to torture by the tyrant for having taken part in a conspiracy, still making no betrayal of her confederates, she at last bit off her tongue and spat it in the tyrant's face, that he might be convinced of the uselessness of his torments, however long they should be continued. Everybody knows what to this day is the great Lacedæmonian solemnity--the διαμαστύγωσις, or scourging; in which sacred rite the Spartan youths are beaten with scourges before the altar, their parents and kinsmen standing by and exhorting them to stand it bravely out. For it will be always counted more honourable and glorious that the soul rather than the body has given itself to stripes. But if so high a value is put on the earthly glory, won by mental and bodily vigour, that men, for the praise of their fellows, I may say, despise the sword, the fire, the cross, the wild beasts, the torture; these surely are but trifling sufferings to obtain a celestial glory and a divine reward. If the bit of glass is so precious, what must the true pearl be worth? Are we not called on, then, most joyfully to lay out as much for the true as others do for the false?

Chapter V

I leave out of account now the motive of glory. All these same cruel and painful conflicts, a mere vanity you find among men--in fact, a sort of mental disease--as trampled under foot.

How many ease-lovers does the conceit of arms give to the sword? They actually go down to meet the very wild beasts in vain ambition; and they fancy themselves more winsome from the bites and scars of the contest. Some have sold themselves to fires, to run a certain distance in a burning tunic. Others, with most enduring shoulders, have walked about under the hunters' whips.

The Lord has given these things a place in the world, O blessed, not without some reason: for what reason, but now to animate us, and on that day to confound us if we have feared to suffer for the truth, that we might be saved, what others out of vanity have eagerly sought for to their ruin?

Chapter VI

Passing, too, from examples of enduring constancy having such an origin as this, let us turn to a simple contemplation of man's estate in its ordinary conditions, that mayhap from things which happen to us whether we will or no, and which we must set our minds to bear, we may get instruction.

How often, then, have fires consumed the living! How often have wild beasts torn men in pieces, it may be in their own forests, or it may be in the heart of cities, when they have chanced to escape from their dens! How many have fallen by the robber's sword! How many have suffered at the hands of enemies the death of the cross, after having been tortured first, yes, and treated with every sort of contumely! One may even suffer in the cause of a man what he hesitates to suffer in the cause of God. In reference to this indeed, let the present time [8969] bear testimony, when so many persons of rank have met with death in a mere human being's cause, and that though from their birth and dignities and bodily condition and age such a fate seemed most unlikely; either suffering at his hands if they have taken part against him, or from his enemies if they have been his partisans.

Footnotes:

8961. Written in his early ministry, and strict orthodoxy. [It may be dated circa a.d. 197, as external evidence will shew.]

8962. Eph. iv. 30. [Some differences had risen between these holy sufferers, as to the personal merits of offenders who had appealed to them for their interest in restoring them to communion.

8963. [He favours this resource as sanctioned by custom, and gently persuades them, by agreeing as to its propriety, to bestow peace upon others.

But, the foresight of those who objected was afterwards justified, for in Cyprian's day this practice led to greater evils, and he was obliged to discourage it (ep. xi.) in an epistle to confessors.]

8964. [Who ministered to their fellow-Christians in prison, for the testimony of Jesus. What follows is a sad picture of social life among heathens.]

8965. Matt. vi. 21.

8966 1 Cor. ix. 25.

8967. Matt. xxvi. 41.

8968. [He is said to have perished circa a.d. 170.]

8969. [After the defeat and suicide of Albinus, at Lyons, many persons, some of Senatorial rank, were cruelly put to death.]

V. Appendix

Introductory Notice to the Martyrdom of Perpetua and Felicitas.
[Translated by the Rev. R. E. Wallis, Ph.D.]

Nobody, will blame me for placing here the touching history of these Martyrs.

It illustrates the period of history we are now considering, and sheds light on the preceding treatise. I can hardly read it without tears, and it ought to make us love "the noble army of martyrs." I think Tertullian was the editor of the story, not its author. [8970] Felicitas is mentioned by name in the De Anima: and the closing paragraph of this memoir is quite in his style. To these words I need only add that Dr. Routh, who unfortunately decided not to re-edit it, ascribes the first edition to Lucas Holstenius.

He was Librarian of the Vatican and died in 1661. The rest may be learned from this Introductory Notice of the Translator:

Perpetua and Felicitas suffered martyrdom in the reign of Septimius Severus, about the year 202 a.d. Tertullian mentions Perpetua, [8971] and a further clue to the date is given in the allusion to the birth-day of "Geta the Cæsar," the son of Septimius Severus.

There is therefore, good reason for rejecting the opinion held by some, that they suffered under Valerian and Gallienus. Some think that they suffered at Tuburbium in Mauritania; but the more general opinion is, that Carthage was the scene of their martyrdom.

The "Acta," detailing the sufferings of Perpetua and Felicitas, has been held by all critics to be a genuine document of antiquity. But much difference exists as to who was the compiler. In the writing itself, Perpetua and Saturus are mentioned as having written certain portions of it; and there is no reason to doubt the statement. Who the writer of the remaining portion was, is not known. Some have assigned the work to Tertullian; some have maintained that, whoever the writer was, he was a Montanist, and some have tried to show that both martyrs and narrator were Montanists.[8972] The narrator must have been a contemporary; according to many critics, he was an eye-witness of the sufferings of the martyrs. And he must have written the narrative shortly after the events.

Dean Milman says, "There appear strong indications that the acts of these African martyrs are translated from the Greek; at least it is difficult otherwise to account for the frequent untranslated Greek words and idioms in the text. [8973]

The Passion of Perpetua and Felicitas was edited by Petrus Possinus, Rome, 1663; by Henr. Valesius, Paris, 1664; and the Bollandists. The best and latest edition is by Ruissart, whose text is adopted in Gallandi's and Migne's collections of the Fathers.

The Passion of the Holy Martyrs Perpetua and Felicitas

Preface [8974]

If ancient illustrations of faith which both testify to God's grace and tend to man's edification are collected in writing, so that by the perusal of them, as if by the reproduction of the facts, as well God may be honoured, as man may be strengthened; why should not new instances be also collected, that shall be equally suitable for both purposes,--if only on the ground that these modern examples will one day become ancient and available for posterity, although in their present time they are esteemed of less authority, by reason of the presumed veneration for antiquity? But let men look to it, if they judge the power of the Holy Spirit to be one, according to the times and seasons; since some things of later date must be esteemed of more account as being nearer to the very last times, in accordance with the exuberance of grace manifested to the final periods determined for the world. For "in the last days, saith the Lord, I will pour out of my Spirit upon all flesh; and their sons and their daughters shall prophesy. And upon my servants and my handmaidens will I pour out of my Spirit; and your young men shall see visions, and your old men shall dream dreams." [8975] And thus we--who both acknowledge and reverence, even as we do the prophecies, modern visions as equally promised to us, and consider the other powers of the Holy Spirit as an agency of the Church for which also He was sent, administering all gifts in all, even as the Lord distributed to every one[8976] as well needfully collect them in writing, as commemorate them in reading to God's glory; that so no weakness or despondency of faith may suppose that the divine grace abode only among the ancients, whether in respect of the condescension that raised up martyrs, or that gave revelations; since God always carries into effect what He has promised, for a testimony to unbelievers, to believers for a benefit.

And we therefore, what we have heard and handled, declare also to you, brethren and little children, that as well you who were concerned in these matters may be reminded of them again to the glory of the Lord, as that you who know them by report may have communion with the blessed martyrs, and through them with the Lord Jesus Christ, to whom be glory and honour, for ever and ever.[8977] Amen.

Chapter I - Argument --When the Saints Were Apprehended, St. Perpetua Successfully Resisted Her Father's Pleading, Was Baptized with the Others, Was Thrust into a Filthy Dungeon. Anxious About Her Infant, by a Vision Granted to Her, She Understood that Her Martyrdom Would Take Place Very Shortly

1. The young catechumens, Revocatus and his fellow-servant Felicitas, Saturninus and Secundulus, were apprehended. And among them also was Vivia Perpetua, respectably born, liberally educated, a married matron, having a father and mother and two brothers, one of whom, like herself, was a catechumen, and a son an infant at the breast. She herself was about twenty-two years of age. From this point onward she shall herself narrate the whole course of her martyrdom, as she left it described by her own hand and with her own mind.

2. "While" says she, "we were still with the persecutors, and my father, for the sake of his affection for me, was persisting in seeking to turn me away, and to cast me down from the faith,--Father,' said I, do you see, let us say, this vessel lying here to be a little pitcher, or something else?' And he said, I see it to be so.' And I replied to him, Can it be called by any other name than what it is?'

And he said, No.' Neither can I call myself anything else than what I am, a Christian.' Then my father, provoked at this saying, threw himself upon me, as if he would tear my eyes out. But he only distressed me, and went away overcome by the devil's arguments. Then, in a few days after I had been without my father, I gave thanks to the Lord; and his absence became a source of consolation [8978] to me. In that same interval of a few days we were baptized, and to me the Spirit prescribed that in the water of baptism nothing else was to be sought for bodily endurance. [8979] After a few days we are taken into the dungeon, and I was very much afraid, because I had never felt such darkness. O terrible day! O the fierce heat of the shock of the soldiery, because of the crowds! I was very unusually distressed by my anxiety for my infant. There were present there Tertius and Pomponius, the blessed deacons who ministered to us, and had arranged by means of a gratuity that we might be refreshed by being sent out for a few hours into a pleasanter part of the prison. Then going out of the dungeon, all attended to their own wants. [8980] I suckled my child, which was now enfeebled with hunger. In my anxiety for it, I addressed my mother and comforted my brother, and commended to their care my son. I was languishing because I had seen them languishing on my account.

Such solicitude I suffered for many days, and I obtained for my infant to remain in the dungeon with me; and forthwith I grew strong and was relieved from distress and anxiety about my infant; and the dungeon became to me as it were a palace, so that I preferred being there to being elsewhere.

3. "Then my brother said to me, My dear sister, you are already in a position of great dignity, and are such that you may ask for a vision, and that it may be made known to you whether this is to result in a passion or an escape.' [8981] And I, who knew that I was privileged to converse with the Lord, whose kindnesses I had found to be so great, boldly promised him, and said, To-morrow I will tell you.' And I asked, and this was what was shown me. I saw a golden ladder of marvellous

height, reaching up even to heaven, and very narrow, so that persons could only ascend it one by one; and on the sides of the ladder was fixed every kind of iron weapon. There were there swords, lances, hooks, daggers; so that if any one went up carelessly, or not looking upwards, he would be torn to pieces and his flesh would cleave to the iron weapons. And under the ladder itself was crouching a dragon of wonderful size, who lay in wait for those who ascended, and frightened them from the ascent. And Saturus went up first, who had subsequently delivered himself up freely on our account, not having been present at the time that we were taken prisoners. And he attained the top of the ladder, and turned towards me, and said to me, Perpetua, I am waiting for [8982] you; but be careful that the dragon do not bite you.' And I said, In the name of the Lord Jesus Christ, he shall not hurt me.' And from under the ladder itself, as if in fear of me, he slowly lifted up his head; and as I trod upon the first step, I trod upon his head. And I went up, and I saw an immense extent of garden, and in the midst of the garden a white-haired man sitting in the dress of a shepherd, [8983] of a large stature, milking sheep; and standing around were many thousand white-robed ones. And he raised his head, and looked upon me, and said to me, Thou art welcome, daughter.' And he called me, and from the cheese as he was milking he gave me as it were a little cake, and I received it with folded hands; and I ate it, and all who stood around said Amen. And at the sound of their voices I was awakened, still tasting a sweetness which I cannot describe. And I immediately related this to my brother, and we understood that it was to be a passion, and we ceased henceforth to have any hope in this world.

Chapter II - Argument. Perpetua, When Besieged by Her Father, Comforts Him. When Led with Others to the Tribunal, She Avows Herself a Christian, and is Condemned with the Rest to the Wild Beasts. She Prays for Her Brother Dinocrates, Who Was Dead

1. "After a few days there prevailed a report that we should be heard. And then my father came to me from the city, worn out with anxiety. He came up to me, that he might cast me down, saying, Have pity my daughter, on my grey hairs. Have pity on your father, if I am worthy to be called a father by you. If with these hands I have brought you up to this flower of your age, if I have preferred you to all your brothers, do not deliver me up to the scorn of men. Have regard to your brothers, have regard to your mother and your aunt, have regard to your son, who will not be able to live after you. Lay aside your courage, and do not bring us all to destruction; for none of us will speak in freedom if you should suffer anything.' These things said my father in his affection, kissing my hands, and throwing himself at my feet; and with tears he called me not Daughter, but Lady. And I grieved over the grey hairs of my father, that he alone of all my family would not rejoice over my passion. And I comforted him, saying, On that scaffold [8984] whatever God wills shall happen. For know that we are not placed in our own power, but in that of God.' And he departed from me in sorrow.

2. "Another day, while we were at dinner, we were suddenly taken away to be heard, and we arrived at the town-hall. At once the rumour spread through the neighbourhood of the public place, and an immense number of people were gathered together.

We mount the platform. The rest were interrogated, and confessed. Then they came to me, and my father immediately appeared with my boy, and withdrew me from the step, and said in a supplicating tone, Have pity on your babe.' And Hilarianus the procurator, who had just received the power of life and death in the place of the proconsul Minucius Timinianus, who was deceased, said, Spare the grey hairs of your father, spare the infancy of your boy, offer sacrifice for the well-being of the emperors.' And I replied, I will not do so.' Hilarianus said, Are you a Christian?' And I replied, I am a Christian.' And as my father stood there to cast me down from the faith, he was ordered by Hilarianus to be thrown down, and was beaten with rods. And my father's misfortune grieved me as if I myself had been beaten, I so grieved for his wretched old age. [8985] The procurator then delivers judgment on all of us, and condemns us to the wild beasts, and we went down cheerfully to the dungeon. Then, because my child had been used to receive suck from me, and to stay with me in the prison, I send Pomponius the deacon to my father to ask for the infant, but my father would not give it him. And even as God willed it, the child no long desired the breast, nor did my breast cause me uneasiness, lest I should be tormented by care for my babe and by the pain of my breasts at once.

3. "After a few days, whilst we were all praying, on a sudden, in the middle of our prayer, there came to me a word, and I named Dinocrates; and I was amazed that that name had never come into my mind until then, and I was grieved as I remembered his misfortune. And I felt myself immediately to be worthy, and to be called on to ask on his behalf. [8986] And for him I began earnestly to make supplication, and to cry with groaning to the Lord. Without delay, on that very night, this was shown to me in a vision. [8987] I saw Dinocrates going out from a gloomy place, where also there were several others, and he was parched and very thirsty, with a filthy countenance and pallid colour, and the wound on his face which he had when he died. This Dinocrates had been my brother after the flesh, seven years of age [8988] who died miserably with disease--his face being so eaten out with cancer, that his death caused repugnance to all men.

For him I had made my prayer, and between him and me there was a large interval, [8989] so that neither of us could approach to the other. And moreover, in the same place where Dinocrates was, there was a pool full of water, having its brink higher than was the stature of the boy; and Dinocrates raised himself up as if to drink. And I was grieved that, although that pool held water, still, on account of the height to its brink, he could not drink. And I was aroused, and knew that my brother was in suffering. But I trusted that my prayer would bring help to his suffering; and I prayed for him every day until we passed over into the prison of the camp, for we were to fight in the camp-show. Then was the birth-day of Geta Cæsar, and I made my prayer for my brother day and night, groaning and weeping that he might be granted to me.

4. "Then, on the day on which we remained in fetters, [8990] this was shown to me. I saw that that place which I had formerly observed to be in gloom was now bright; and Dinocrates, with a clean body well clad, was finding refreshment. And where there had been a wound, I saw a scar; and that pool which I had before seen, I saw now with its margin lowered even to the boy's navel. And one drew water from the pool incessantly, and upon its brink was a goblet filled with water; and Dinocrates drew near and began to drink from it, and the goblet did not fail. And when he was satisfied, he went away from the water to play joyously, after the manner of children, and I awoke. Then I understood that he was translated from the place of punishment.

Chapter III - Argument. Perpetua is Again Tempted by Her Father. Her Third Vision, Wherein She is Led Away to Struggle Against an Egyptian. She Fights, Conquers, and Receives the Reward

1. "Again, after a few days, Pudens, a soldier, an assistant overseer [8991] of the prison, who began to regard us in great esteem, perceiving that the great power of God was in us, admitted many brethren to see us, that both we and they might be mutually refreshed. And when the day of the exhibition drew near, my father, worn with suffering, came in to me, and began to tear out his beard, and to throw himself on the earth, and to cast himself down on his face, and to reproach his years, and to utter such words as might move all creation. I grieved for his unhappy old age. [8992]

2. "The day before that on which we were to fight, I saw in a vision that Pomponius the deacon came hither to the gate of the prison, and knocked vehemently. I went out to him, and opened the gate for him; and he was clothed in a richly ornamented white robe, and he had on manifold calliculæ. [8993] And he said to me, Perpetua, we are waiting for you; come!' And he held his hand to me, and we began to go through rough and winding places. Scarcely at length had we arrived breathless at the amphitheatre, when he led me into the middle of the arena, and said to me, Do not fear, I am here with you, and I am labouring with you;' and he departed. And I gazed upon an immense assembly in astonishment. And because I knew that I was given to the wild beasts, I marvelled that the wild beasts were not let loose upon me. Then there came forth against me a certain Egyptian, horrible in appearance, with his backers, to fight with me. And there came to me, as my helpers and encouragers, handsome youths; and I was stripped, and became a man. [8994] Then my helpers began to rub me with oil, as is the custom for contest; and I beheld that Egyptian on the other hand rolling in the dust. [8995] And a certain man came forth, of wondrous height, so that he even over-topped the top of the amphitheatre; and he wore a loose tunic and a purple robe between two bands over the middle of the breast; and he had on calliculæ of varied form, made of gold and silver; and he carried a rod, as if he were a trainer of gladiators, and a green branch upon which were apples of gold. And he called for silence, and said, This Egyptian, if he should overcome this

woman, shall kill her with the sword; and if she shall conquer him, she shall receive this branch.' Then he departed. And we drew near to one another, and began to deal out blows. He sought to lay hold of my feet, while I struck at his face with my heels; and I was lifted up in the air, and began thus to thrust at him as if spurning the earth. But when I saw that there was some delay I joined my hands so as to twine my fingers with one another; and I took hold upon his head, and he fell on his face, and I trod upon his head. [8996] And the people began to shout, and my backers to exult. And I drew near to the trainer and took the branch; and he kissed me, and said to me, Daughter, peace be with you:' and I began to go gloriously to the Sanavivarian gate. [8997] Then I awoke, and perceived that I was not to fight with beasts, but against the devil.

Still I knew that the victory was awaiting me. This, so far, I have completed several days before the exhibition; but what passed at the exhibition itself let who will write."

Chapter IV - Argument. Saturus, in a Vision, and Perpetua Being Carried by Angels into the Great Light, Behold the Martyrs. Being Brought to the Throne of God, are Received with a Kiss. They Reconcile Optatus the Bishop and Aspasius the Presbyter

1. Moreover, also, the blessed Saturus related this his vision, which he himself committed to writing:--"We had suffered," says he, "and we were gone forth from the flesh, and we were beginning to be borne by four angels into the east; and their hands touched us not. And we floated not supine, looking upwards, but as if ascending a gentle slope. And being set free, we at length saw the first boundless light; and I said, Perpetua' (for she was at my side), this is what the Lord promised to us; we have received the promise.' And while we are borne by those same four angels, there appears to us a vast space which was like a pleasure-garden, having rose-trees and every kind of flower. And the height of the trees was after the measure of a cypress, and their leaves were falling[8998] incessantly. Moreover, there in the pleasure-garden four other angels appeared, brighter than the previous ones, who, when they saw us, gave us honour, and said to the rest of the angels, Here they are! Here they are!' with admiration. And those four angels who bore us, being greatly afraid, put us down; and we passed over on foot the space of a furlong in a broad path. There we found Jocundus and Saturninus and Artaxius, who having suffered the same persecution were burnt alive; and Quintus, who also himself a martyr had departed in the prison. And we asked of them where the rest were. And the angels said to us, Come first, enter and greet your Lord.'

2. "And we came near to place, the walls of which were such as if they were built of light; and before the gate of that place stood four angels, who clothed those who entered with white robes. And being clothed, we entered and saw the boundless light, and heard the united voice of some who said without ceasing, Holy! Holy! Holy!' [8999] And in the midst of that place we saw as it were a hoary man sitting, having snow-white hair, and with a youthful countenance; and his feet we saw not.

And on his right hand and on his left were four-and-twenty elders, and behind them a great many others were standing.

We entered with great wonder, and stood before the throne; and the four angels raised us up, and we kissed Him, and He passed His hand over our face. And the rest of the elders said to us, Let us stand;' and we stood and made peace. And the elders said to us, Go and enjoy.' And I said, Perpetua, you have what you wish.' And she said to me, Thanks be to God, that joyous as I was in the flesh, I am now more joyous here.'

3. "And we went forth, and saw before the entrance Optatus the bishop at the right hand, and Aspasius the presbyter, a teacher, [9000] at the left hand, separate and sad; and they cast themselves at our feet, and said to us, Restore peace between us, because you have gone forth and have left us thus.' And we said to them, Art not thou our father, and thou our presbyter, that you should cast yourselves at our feet?' And we prostrated ourselves, and we embraced them; and Perpetua began to speak with them, and we drew them apart in the pleasure-garden under a rose-tree.

And while we were speaking with them, the angels said unto them, Let them alone, that they may refresh themselves; [9001] and if you have any dissensions between you, forgive one another.' And they drove them away. And they said to Optatus, Rebuke thy people, because they assemble to you as if returning from the circus, and contending about factious matters.' And then it seemed to us as if they would shut the doors.

And in that place we began to recognise many brethren, and moreover martyrs. We were all nourished with an indescribable odour, which satisfied us.

Then, I joyously awoke."

Chapter V - Argument. Secundulus Dies in the Prison. Felicitas is Pregnant, But with Many Prayers She Brings Forth in the Eighth Month Without Suffering, the Courage of Perpetua and of Saturus Unbroken

1. The above were the more eminent visions of the blessed martyrs Saturus and Perpetua themselves, which they themselves committed to writing. [9002] But God called Secundulus, while he has yet in the prison, by an earlier exit from the world, not without favour, so as to give a respite to the beasts.

Nevertheless, even if his soul did not acknowledge cause for thankfulness, assuredly his flesh did.

2. But respecting Felicitas (for to her also the Lord's favour approached in the same way), when she had already gone eight months with child (for she had been pregnant when she was apprehended), as the day of the exhibition was drawing near, she was in great grief lest on account of her pregnancy she should be delayed,--because pregnant women are not allowed to be publicly punished,--and lest she should shed her sacred and guiltless blood among some who had been wicked subsequently. Moreover, also, her fellow-martyrs were painfully saddened lest they should leave so excellent a friend, and as it were companion, alone in the path of the same hope. Therefore, joining together their united cry, they poured forth their prayer to the Lord three days before the exhibition. Immediately after their prayer her pains came upon her, and when, with the difficulty natural to an eight months' delivery, in the labour of bringing forth she was sorrowing, some one of the servants of the Cataractarii [9003] said to her, "You who are in such suffering now, what will you do when you are thrown to the beasts, which you despised when you refused to sacrifice?"

And she replied, "Now it is I that suffer what I suffer; but then there will be another in me, who will suffer for me, because I also am about to suffer for Him." Thus she brought forth a little girl, which a certain sister brought up as her daughter.

3. Since then the Holy Spirit permitted, and by permitting willed, that the proceedings of that exhibition should be committed to writing, although we are unworthy to complete the description of so great a glory; yet we obey as it were the command of the most blessed Perpetua, nay her sacred trust, and add one more testimony concerning her constancy and her loftiness of mind. While they were treated with more severity by the tribune, because, from the intimations of certain deceitful men, he feared lest they should be withdrawn from the prison by some sort of magic incantations, Perpetua answered to his face, and said, "Why do you not at least permit us to be refreshed, being as we are objectionable to the most noble Cæsar, and having to fight on his birth-day? [9004] Or is it not your glory if we are brought forward fatter on that occasion?" The tribune shuddered and blushed, and commanded that they should be kept with more humanity, so that permission was given to their brethren and others to go in and be refreshed with them; even the keeper of the prison trusting them now himself.

4. Moreover, on the day before, when in that last meal, which they call the free meal, they were partaking as far as they could, not of a free supper, but of an ἀγάπη; with the same firmness they were uttering such words as these to the people, denouncing against them the judgment of the Lord, bearing witness to the felicity of their passion, laughing at the curiosity of the people who came together; while Saturus said, "To-morrow is not enough for you, for you to behold with pleasure that which you hate.

Friends today, enemies to-morrow.

Yet note our faces diligently, that you may recognise them on that day of judgment." Thus all departed thence astonished, and from these things many believed.

Chapter VI - Argument. From the Prison They are Led Forth with Joy into the Amphitheatre, Especially Perpetua and Felicitas. All Refuse to Put on Profane Garments. They are Scourged, They are Thrown to the Wild Beasts. Saturus Twice is Unhurt. Perpetua and Felicitas are Thrown Down; They are Called Back to the Sanavivarian Gate. Saturus Wounded by a Leopard, Exhorts the Soldier. They Kiss One Another, and are Slain with the Sword

1. The day of their victory shone forth, and they proceeded from the prison into the amphitheatre, as if to an assembly, joyous and of brilliant countenances; if perchance shrinking, it was with joy, and not with fear. Perpetua followed with placid look, and with step and gait as a matron of Christ, beloved of God; casting down the luster of her eyes from the gaze of all. Moreover, Felicitas, rejoicing that she had safely brought forth, so that she might fight with the wild beasts; from the blood and from the midwife to the gladiator, to wash after childbirth with a second baptism. And when they were brought to the gate, and were constrained to put on the clothing--the men, that of the priests of Saturn, and the women, that of those who were consecrated to Ceres--that noble-minded woman resisted even to the end with constancy. For she said, "We have come thus far of our own accord, for this reason, that our liberty might not be restrained. For this reason we have yielded our minds, that we might not do any such thing as this: we have agreed on this with you."

Injustice acknowledged the justice; the tribune yielded to their being brought as simply as they were. Perpetua sang psalms, already treading under foot the head of the Egyptian; Revocatus, and Saturninus, and Saturus uttered threatenings against the gazing people about this martyrdom. When they came within sight of Hilarianus, by gesture and nod, they began to say to Hilarianus, "Thou judgest us," say they, "but God will judge thee." At this the people, exasperated, demanded that they should be tormented with scourges as they passed along the rank of the venators. [9005] And they indeed rejoiced that they should have incurred any one of their Lord's passions.

2. But He who had said, "Ask, and ye shall receive," [9006] gave to them when they asked, that death which each one had wished for. For when at any time they had been discoursing among themselves about their wish in respect of their martyrdom, Saturninus indeed had professed that he wished that he might be thrown to all the beasts; doubtless that he might wear a more glorious crown. Therefore in the beginning of the exhibition he and Revocatus made trial of the leopard, and moreover upon the scaffold they were harassed by the bear. Saturus, however, held nothing in greater abomination than a bear; but he imagined that he would be put an end to with one bite of a leopard. Therefore, when a wild boar was supplied, it was the huntsman rather who had supplied that boar who was gored by that same beast, and died the day after the shows.

Saturus only was drawn out; and when he had been bound on the floor near to a bear, the bear would not come forth from his den. And so Saturus for the second time is recalled unhurt.

3. Moreover, for the young women the devil prepared a very fierce cow, provided especially for that purpose contrary to custom, rivalling their sex also in that of the beasts. And so, stripped and clothed with nets, they were led forth. The populace shuddered as they saw one young woman of delicate frame, and another with breasts still dropping from her recent childbirth. So, being recalled, they are unbound. [9007] Perpetua is first led in. She was tossed, and fell on her loins; and when she saw her tunic torn from her side, she drew it over her as a veil for her middle, rather mindful of her modesty than her suffering. Then she was called for again, and bound up her dishevelled hair; for it was not becoming for a martyr to suffer with dishevelled hair, lest she should appear to be mourning in her glory. So she rose up; and when she saw Felicitas crushed, she approached and gave her her hand, and lifted her up. And both of them stood together; and the brutality of the populace being appeased, they were recalled to the Sanavivarian gate. Then Perpetua was received by a certain one who was still a catechumen, Rusticus by name, who kept

close to her; and she, as if aroused from sleep, so deeply had she been in the Spirit and in an ecstasy, began to look round her, and to say to the amazement of all, "I cannot tell when we are to be led out to that cow." And when she had heard what had already happened, she did not believe it [9008] until she had perceived certain signs of injury in her body and in her dress, and had recognised the catechumen.

Afterwards causing that catechumen and the brother to approach, she addressed them, saying, "Stand fast in the faith, and love one another, all of you, and be not offended at my sufferings."

4. The same Saturus at the other entrance exhorted the soldier Pudens, saying, "Assuredly here I am, as I have promised and foretold, for up to this moment I have felt no beast. And now believe with your whole heart. Lo, I am going forth to that beast, and I shall be destroyed with one bite of the leopard." And immediately at the conclusion of the exhibition he was thrown to the leopard; and with one bite of his he was bathed with such a quantity of blood, that the people shouted out to him as he was returning, the testimony of his second baptism, "Saved and washed, saved and washed." [9009] Manifestly he was assuredly saved who had been glorified in such a spectacle. Then to the soldier Pudens he said, "Farewell, and be mindful of my faith; and let not these things disturb, but confirm you."

And at the same time he asked for a little ring from his finger, and returned it to him bathed in his wound, leaving to him an inherited token and the memory of his blood. And then lifeless he is cast down with the rest, to be slaughtered in the usual place. And when the populace called for them into the midst, that as the sword penetrated into their body they might make their eyes partners in the murder, they rose up of their own accord, and transferred themselves whither the people wished; but they first kissed one another, that they might consummate their martyrdom with the kiss of peace. The rest indeed, immoveable and in silence, received the sword-thrust; much more Saturus, who also had first ascended the ladder, and first gave up his spirit, for he also was waiting for Perpetua. But Perpetua, that she might taste some pain, being pierced between the ribs, cried out loudly, and she herself placed the wavering right hand of the youthful gladiator to her throat. [9010] Possibly such a woman could not have been slain unless she herself had willed it, because she was feared by the impure spirit.

O most brave and blessed martyrs! O truly called and chosen unto the glory of our Lord Jesus Christ! whom whoever magnifies, and honours, and adores, assuredly ought to read these examples for the edification of the Church, not less than the ancient ones, so that new virtues also may testify that one and the same Holy Spirit is always operating even until now, and God the Father Omnipotent, and His Son Jesus Christ our Lord, whose is the glory and infinite power for ever and ever.

Amen.

Elucidations

(Dinocrates, cap. ii)

The avidity with which the Latin controversial writers seize upon this fanciful passage, (which, in fact, is subversive of their whole doctrine about Purgatory, as is the text from the Maccabees) makes emphatic the utter absence from the early Fathers of any reference to such a dogma; which, had it existed, must have appeared in every reference to the State of the Dead, and in every account of the discipline of penitents.

Arbp. Usher [9011] ingeniously turns the tables upon these errorists, by quoting the Prayers for the Dead, which were used in the Early Church, but which, such as they were, not only make no mention of a Purgatory, but refute the dogma, by their uniform limitation of such prayers to the blessed dead, and to their consummation of bliss at the Last day and not before.

Such a prayer seems to occur in 2 Tim. i. 18. The context (vers. 16-18, and iv. 19) strongly supports this view; Onesiphorus is spoken of as if deceased, apparently. But, as Chrysostom understands it, he was only absent (in Rome) from his household.

From i. 17 we should infer that he had left Rome. [9012]

Footnotes:

8970. Cap. lv. He calls her fortissima martyr, and she is one of only two or three contemporary sufferers whom he mentioned by name.

8971. [In the De Anima, cap. lv. as see above.]

8972. [Yet see the sermons of St. Augustine (if indeed his) on the Passion of these Saints. Sermon 281 and 282, opp. Tom. v. pp. 1284-5.]

8973. Hist. of Christianity, vol. i. ch. viii.

8974. [Both Perpetua and Felicitas were evidently Montanistic in character and impressions, but, the fact that they have never been reputed other than Catholic, goes far to explain Tertullian's position for years after he had withdrawn from communion with the vacillating Victor.]

8975. Joel ii. 28, 29. [The quotation here is a note of Montanistic prepossessions in the writer.]

8976. [Routh notes this as undoubted evidence of a Montanistic author.

Reliquiæ, Vol. I. p. 455.]

8977. [St. Augustine takes pains to remind us that these Acta are not canonical. De Anima, cap. 2, opp. Tom. x. p. 481.]

8978. "Refrigeravit," Græce ἀνέπαυσεν, scil. "requiem dedit."

8979. i.e. the grace of martyrdom.

8980. Sibi vacabant.

8981. Commeatus.

8982. "Sustineo," Græce ὑπομένω, scil. "exspecto."

8983. This was an ordinary mode of picturing our Lord in the oratories and on the sacred vessels of those days. [This passage will recall the allegory of Hermas, with which the martyr was doubtless familiar.]

8984. "Catasta," a raised platform on which the martyrs were placed either for trial or torture.

8985. [St. August. opp. iv. 541.]

8986. [The story in 2 Maccab. xii. 40-45, is there narrated as a thought suggested to the soldiers under Judas, and not discouraged by him, though it concerned men guilty of idolatry and dying in mortal sin, by the vengeance of God. It may have occurred to early Christians that their heathen kindred might, therefore, not be beyond the visitations of the Divine compassion.

But, obviously, even were it not an Apocryphal text, it can have no bearing whatever on the case of Christians.

The doctrine of Purgatory is that nobody dying in mortal sin can have the benefit of its discipline, or any share in the prayers and oblations of the Faithful, whatever.]

8987. "Oromate." [This vision, it must be observed, has nothing to do with prayers for the Christian dead, for this brother of Perpetua was a heathen child whom she supposed to be in the Inferi. It illustrates the anxieties Christians felt for those of their kindred who had not died in the Lord; even for children of seven years of age. Could the gulf be bridged and they received into Abraham's bosom?

This dream of Perpetua comforted her with a trust that so it should be. Of course this story has been used fraudulently, to

help a system of which these times knew nothing. Cyprian says expressly: "Apud Inferos confessio, non est, nec ἐξομολόγησις illic fieri potest." Epistola lii. p. 98. Opp. Paris, 1574. In the Edinburgh series (translation) this epistle is numbered 51, and elsewhere 54.]

8988. [There is not the slightest reason to suppose that this child had been baptized: the father a heathen and Perpetua herself a recent catechumen. Elucidation.]

8989. "Diadema," or rather "diastema." [Borrowed from Luke xvi. 26. But that gulf could not be passed according to the evangelist.]

8990. "Nervo."

8991. Optio.

8992. [St. Aug. Opp. Tom. v. p. 1284.]

8993. It seems uncertain what may be the meaning of this word. It is variously supposed to signify little round ornaments either of cloth or metal attached to the soldier's dress, or the small bells on the priestly robe. Some also read the word galliculæ, small sandals.

8994. [Concerning these visions, see Augustine, De Anima, cap. xviii. el seq.]

8995. "Afa" is the Greek word ἀφή, a grip; hence used of the yellow sand sprinkled over wrestlers, to enable them to grasp one another.

8996. [Ps. xliv. 5. Also lx. 12; xci. 13; cviii. 13.]

8997. This was the way by which the victims spared by the popular clemency escaped from the amphitheatre.

8998. "Cadebant;" but "ardebant"--"were burning"--seems a more probable reading. [The imitations of the Shepherd of Hermas, in this memoir hardly need pointing out.]

8999. Agios.

9000. A presbyter, that is, whose office was to teach, as distinct from other presbyters. See Cyprian, Epistles, vol. i. Ep. xxiii. p. 68. note i. transl. [One of those referred to by St. James iii. 1, and by St. Paul, 1 Tim. v. 17.]

9001. More probably, "rest and refresh yourselves." ["Go and enjoy," or, "play," or "take pleasure," in the section preceding.]

9002. [To be regarded like the Shepherd of Hermas, merely as visions, or allegorical romances.]

9003. "The gaolers," so called from the "cataracta," or prison-gate, which they guarded.

9004. [A gentle banter, like that of St. Lawrence on the gridiron.]

9005. A row of men drawn up to scourge them as they passed along, a punishment probably similar to what is called "running the gauntlet."

9006. John xvi. 24.

9007. Ita revocatæ discinguntur. Dean Milmam prefers reading this, "Thus recalled, they are clad in loose robes."

9008. [Routh, Reliq. Vol. I. p. 360.]

9009. A cry in mockery of what was known as the effect of Christian baptism.

9010. [Routh, Reliquiæ, Vol. I. p. 358.]

9011. Republished, Oxford, 1838.

9012. See Opp. Tom. xi. p. 657. Ed. Migne.

VI - Of Patience [9013]

[Translated by the Rev. S. Thelwall.]

Chapter I - Of Patience Generally; And Tertullian's Own Unworthiness to Treat of It

I fully confess unto the Lord God that it has been rash enough, if not even impudent, in me to have dared compose a treatise on Patience, for practising which I am all unfit, being a man of no goodness; [9014] whereas it were becoming that such as have addressed themselves to the demonstration and commendation of some particular thing, should themselves first be conspicuous in the practice of that thing, and should regulate the constancy of their commonishing by the authority of their personal conduct, for fear their words blush at the deficiency of their deeds. And would that this "blushing" would bring a remedy, so that shame for not exhibiting that which we go to suggest to others should prove a tutorship into exhibiting it; except that the magnitude of some good things--just as of some ills too--is insupportable, so that only the grace of divine inspiration is effectual for attaining and practising them.

For what is most good rests most with God; nor does any other than He who possesses it dispense it, as He deems meet to each. And so to discuss about that which it is not given one to enjoy, will be, as it were, a solace; after the manner of invalids, who since they are without health, know not how to be silent about its blessings. So I, most miserable, ever sick with the heats of impatience, must of necessity sigh after, and invoke, and persistently plead for, that health of patience which I possess not; while I recall to mind, and, in the contemplation of my own weakness, digest, the truth, that the good health of faith, and the soundness of the Lord's discipline, accrue not easily to any unless patience sit by his side. [9015] So is patience set over the things of God, that one can obey no precept, fulfil no work well-pleasing to the Lord, if estranged from it. The good of it, even they who live outside it, [9016] honour with the name of highest virtue.

Philosophers indeed, who are accounted animals of some considerable wisdom, assign it so high a place, that, while they are mutually at discord with the various fancies of their sects and rivalries of their sentiments, yet, having a community of regard for patience alone, to this one of their pursuits they have joined in granting peace: for it they conspire; for it they league; it, in their affectation of [9017] virtue, they unanimously pursue; concerning patience they exhibit all their ostentation of wisdom. Grand testimony this is to it, in that it incites even the vain schools of the world[9018] unto praise and glory! Or is it rather an injury, in that a thing divine is bandied among worldly sciences? But let them look to that, who shall presently be ashamed of their wisdom, destroyed and disgraced together with the world [9019] (it lives in).

Chapter II - God Himself an Example of Patience

To us [9020] no human affectation of canine [9021] equanimity, modelled [9022] by insensibility, furnishes the warrant for exercising patience; but the divine arrangement of a living and celestial discipline, holding up before us God Himself in the very first place as an example of patience; who scatters equally over just and unjust the bloom of this light; who suffers the good offices of the seasons, the services of the elements, the tributes of entire nature, to accrue at once to worthy and unworthy; bearing with the most ungrateful nations, adoring as they do the toys of the arts and the works of their own hands, persecuting His Name together with His family; bearing with luxury, avarice, iniquity, malignity, waxing insolent daily: [9023] so that by His own patience He disparages Himself; for the cause why many believe not in the Lord is that they are so long without knowing[9024] that He is wroth with the world. [9025]

Chapter III - Jesus Christ in His Incarnation and Work a More Imitable Example Thereof

And this species of the divine patience indeed being, as it were, at a distance, may perhaps be esteemed as among "things too high for us;" [9026] but what is that which, in a certain way, has been grasped by hand [9027] among men openly on the earth? God suffers Himself to be conceived in a mother's womb, and awaits the time for birth; and, when born, bears the delay of growing up; and, when grown up, is not eager to be recognised, but is furthermore contumelious to Himself, and is baptized by His own servant; and repels with words alone the assaults of the tempter; while from being "Lord" He becomes "Master," teaching man to escape death, having been trained to the exercise of the absolute forbearance of offended patience. [9028] He did not strive; He did not cry aloud; nor did any hear His voice in the streets.

He did not break the bruised reed; the smoking flax He did not quench: for the prophet--nay, the attestation of God Himself, placing His own Spirit, together with patience in its entirety, in His Son--had not falsely spoken. There was none desirous of cleaving to Him whom He did not receive. No one's table or roof did He despise: indeed, Himself ministered to the washing of the disciples' feet; not sinners, not publicans, did He repel; not with that city even which had refused to receive Him was He wroth, [9029] when even the disciples had wished that the celestial fires should be forthwith hurled on so contumelious a town. He cared for the ungrateful; He yielded to His ensnarers. This were a small matter, if He had not had in His company even His own betrayer, and stedfastly abstained from pointing him out. Moreover, while He is being betrayed, while He is being led up "as a sheep for a victim," (for "so He no more opens His mouth than a lamb under the power of the shearer,")He to whom, had He willed it, legions of angels would at one word have presented themselves from the heavens, approved not the avenging sword of even one disciple. The patience of the Lord was wounded in (the wound of) Malchus. And so, too, He cursed for the time to come the works of the sword; and, by the restoration of health, made satisfaction to him whom Himself had not hurt, through Patience, the mother of Mercy. I pass by in silence (the fact) that He is crucified, for this was the end for which He had come; yet had the death which must be undergone need of contumelies likewise? [9030] Nay, but, when about to depart, He wished to be sated with the pleasure of patience. He is spitted on, scourged, derided, clad foully, more foully crowned. Wondrous is the faith of equanimity!

He who had set before Him the concealing of Himself in man's shape, imitated nought of man's impatience! Hence, even more than from any other trait, ought ye, Pharisees, to have recognised the Lord. Patience of this kind none of men would achieve. Such and so mighty evidences--the very magnitude of which proves to be among the nations indeed a cause for rejection of the faith, but among us its reason and rearing--proves manifestly enough (not by the sermons only, in enjoining, but likewise by the sufferings of the Lord in enduring) to them to whom it is given to believe, that as the effect and excellence of some inherent propriety, patience is God's nature.

Chapter IV - Duty of Imitating Our Master Taught Us by Slaves. Even by Beasts. Obedient Imitation is Founded on Patience

Therefore, if we see all servants of probity and right feeling shaping their conduct suitably to the disposition of their lord; if, that is, the art of deserving favour is obedience, [9031] while the rule of obedience is a compliant subjection: how much more does it behove us to be found with a character in accordance with our Lord,--servants as we are of the living God, whose judgment on His servants turns not on a fetter or a cap of freedom, but on an eternity either of penalty or of salvation; for the shunning of which severity or the courting of which liberality there needs a diligence in obedience [9032] as great as are the comminations themselves which the severity utters, or the promises which the liberality freely makes. [9033] And yet we exact obedience [9034] not from men only, who have the bond of their slavery under their chin, [9035] or in any other legal way are debtors to obedience, [9036] but even from cattle, [9037] even from brutes; [9038] understanding that they have been provided and delivered for our uses by the Lord. Shall, then, creatures which God makes subject to us be better than we in the discipline of obedience? [9039] Finally, (the creatures) which obey, acknowledge their masters. Do we hesitate to listen diligently to Him to whom alone we are subjected--that is, the Lord?

But how unjust is it, how ungrateful likewise, not to repay from yourself the same which, through the indulgence of your neighbour, you obtain from others, to him through whom you obtain it!

Nor needs there more words on the exhibition of obedience [9040] due from us to the Lord God; for the acknowledgment [9041] of God understands what is incumbent on it.

Lest, however, we seem to have inserted remarks on obedience [9042] as something irrelevant, (let us remember) that obedience [9043] itself is drawn from patience. Never does an impatient man render it, or a patient fail to find pleasure [9044] in it. Who, then, could treat largely (enough) of the good of that patience which the Lord God, the Demonstrator and Acceptor of all good things, carried about in His own self? [9045] To whom, again, would it be doubtful that every good thing ought, because it pertains [9046] to God, to be earnestly pursued with the whole mind by such as pertain to God? By means of which (considerations) both commendation and exhortation[9047] on the subject of patience are briefly, and as it were in the compendium of a prescriptive rule, established.[9048]

Chapter V - As God is the Author of Patience So the Devil is of Impatience

Nevertheless, the proceeding [9049] of a discussion on the necessaries of faith is not idle, because it is not unfruitful. In edification no loquacity is base, if it be base at any time. [9050] And so, if the discourse be concerning some particular good, the subject requires us to review also the contrary of that good. For you will throw more light on what is to be pursued, if you first give a digest of what is to be avoided.

Let us therefore consider, concerning Impatience, whether just as patience in God, so its adversary quality have been born and detected in our adversary, that from this consideration may appear how primarily adverse it is to faith. For that which has been conceived by God's rival, of course is not friendly to God's things. The discord of things is the same as the discord of their authors. Further, since God is best, the devil on the contrary worst, of beings, by their own very diversity they testify that neither works for [9051] the other; so that anything of good can no more seem to be effected for us by the Evil One, than anything of evil by the Good. Therefore I detect the nativity of impatience in the devil himself, at that very time when he impatiently bore that the Lord God subjected the universal works which He had made to His own image, that is, to man. [9052] For if he had endured (that), he would not have grieved; nor would he have envied man if he had not grieved. Accordingly he deceived him, because he had envied him; but he had envied because he had grieved: he had grieved because, of course, he had not patiently borne. What that angel of perdition[9053] first was--malicious or impatient--I scorn to inquire: since manifest it is that either impatience took its rise together with malice, or else malice from impatience; that subsequently they conspired between themselves; and that they grew up indivisible in one paternal bosom. But, however, having been instructed, by his own experiment, what an aid unto sinning was that which he had been the first to feel, and by means of which he had entered on his course of delinquency, he called the same to his assistance for the thrusting of man into crime. The woman, [9054] immediately on being met by him--I may say so without rashness--was, through his very speech with her, breathed on by a spirit infected with impatience: so certain is it that she would never have sinned at all, if she had honoured the divine edict by maintaining her patience to the end. What (of the fact) that she endured not to have been met alone; but in the presence of Adam, not yet her husband, not yet bound to lend her his ears, [9055] she is impatient of keeping silence, and makes him the transmitter of that which she had imbibed from the Evil One?

Therefore another human being, too, perishes through the impatience of the one; presently, too, perishes of himself, through his own impatience committed in each respect, both in regard of God's premonition and in regard of the devil's cheatery; not enduring to observe the former nor to refute the latter. Hence, whence (the origin) of delinquency, arose the first origin of judgment; hence, whence man was induced to offend, God began to be wroth. Whence (came) the first indignation in God, thence (came) His first patience; who, content at that time with malediction only, refrained in the devil's case from the instant infliction [9056] of punishment. Else what crime, before this guilt of impatience, is imputed to man?

Innocent he was, and in intimate friendship with God, and the husbandman [9057] of paradise. But when once he succumbed to impatience, he quite ceased to be of sweet savour [9058] to God; he quite ceased to be able to endure things celestial. Thenceforward, a creature [9059] given to earth, and ejected from the sight of God, he begins to be easily turned by impatience unto every use offensive to God. For straightway that impatience conceived of the devil's seed, produced, in the fecundity of malice, anger as her son; and when brought forth, trained him in her own arts. For that very thing which had immersed Adam and Eve in death, taught their son, too, to begin with murder. It would be idle for me to ascribe this to impatience, if Cain, that first homicide and first fratricide, had borne with equanimity and not impatiently the refusal by the Lord of his own oblations--if he is not wroth with his own brother--if, finally, he took away no one's life. Since, then, he could neither have killed unless he had been wroth, nor have been wroth unless he had been impatient, he demonstrates that what he did through wrath must be referred to that by which wrath was suggested during this cradle-time of impatience, then (in a certain sense) in her infancy.

But how great presently were her augmentations! And no wonder, If she has been the first delinquent, it is a consequence that, because she has been the first, therefore she is the only parent stem,[9060] too, to every delinquency, pouring down from her own fount various veins of crimes.[9061] Of murder we have spoken; but, being from the very beginning the outcome of anger,[9062] whatever causes besides it shortly found for itself it lays collectively on the account of impatience, as to its own origin.

For whether from private enmities, or for the sake of prey, any one perpetrates that wickedness, [9063] the earlier step is his becoming impatient of [9064] either the hatred or the avarice. Whatever compels a man, it is not possible that without impatience of itself it can be perfected in deed. Who ever committed adultery without impatience of lust? Moreover, if in females the sale of their modesty is forced by the price, of course it is by impatience of contemning gain[9065] that this sale is regulated. [9066] These (I mention) as the principal delinquencies in the sight of the Lord, [9067] for, to speak compendiously, every sin is ascribable to impatience. "Evil" is "impatience of good." None immodest is not impatient of modesty; dishonest of honesty; impious of piety; [9068] unquiet of quietness. In order that each individual may become evil he will be unable to persevere [9069] in being good. How, therefore, can such a hydra of delinquencies fail to offend the Lord, the Disapprover of evils? Is it not manifest that it was through impatience that Israel himself also always failed in his duty toward God, from that time when, [9070] forgetful of the heavenly arm whereby he had been drawn out of his Egyptian affliction, he demands from Aaron "gods [9071] as his guides;" when he pours down for an idol the contributions of his gold: for the so necessary delays of Moses, while he met with God, he had borne with impatience. After the edible rain of the manna, after the watery following [9072] of the rock, they despair of the Lord in not enduring a three-days' thirst; [9073] for this also is laid to their charge by the Lord as impatience. And--not to rove through individual cases-- there was no instance in which it was not by failing in duty through impatience that they perished. How, moreover, did they lay hands on the prophets, except through impatience of hearing them? on the Lord moreover Himself, through impatience likewise of seeing Him? But had they entered the path of patience, they would have been set free. [9074]

Chapter VI - Patience Both Antecedent and Subsequent to Faith

Accordingly it is patience which is both subsequent and antecedent to faith. In short, Abraham believed God, and was accredited by Him with righteousness; [9075] but it was patience which proved his faith, when he was bidden to immolate his son, with a view to (I would not say the temptation, but) the typical attestation of his faith. But God knew whom He had accredited with righteousness. [9076] So heavy a precept, the perfect execution whereof was not even pleasing to the Lord, he patiently both heard, and (if God had willed) would have fulfilled. Deservedly then was he "blessed," because he was "faithful;" deservedly "faithful," because "patient." So faith, illumined by patience, when it was becoming propagated among the nations through "Abraham's seed, which is Christ," [9077] and was superinducing grace over the law, [9078] made patience her pre-eminent coadjutrix for amplifying and fulfilling the law, because that alone had been lacking unto the doctrine of righteousness. For men were of old wont to require "eye for eye, and tooth for tooth"[9079] and to repay with usury "evil with evil;" for, as yet, patience was not on earth, because faith was not either. Of course, meantime, impatience used to enjoy the opportunities which the law gave. That was easy, while the Lord and Master of patience was absent. But after He has supervened, and has united [9080] the grace of faith with patience, now it is no longer lawful to assail even with word, nor to say "fool" [9081] even, without "danger of the judgment."

Anger has been prohibited, our spirits retained, the petulance of the hand checked, the poison of the tongue [9082] extracted. The law has found more than it has lost, while Christ says, "Love your personal enemies, and bless your cursers, and pray for your persecutors, that ye may be sons of your heavenly Father." [9083] Do you see whom patience gains for us as a Father? In this principal precept the universal discipline of patience is succinctly comprised, since evil-doing is not conceded even when it is deserved.

Chapter VII - The Causes of Impatience, and Their Correspondent Precepts

Now, however, while we run through the causes of impatience, all the other precepts also will answer in their own places. If our spirit is aroused by the loss of property, it is commonished by the Lord's Scriptures, in almost every place, to a contemning of the world; [9084] nor is there any more powerful exhortation to contempt of money submitted [9085] (to us), than (the fact) the Lord Himself is found amid no riches. He always justifies the poor, fore-condemns the rich. So He fore-ministered to patience "loss," and to opulence "contempt" (as portion); [9086] demonstrating, by means of (His own) repudiation of riches, that hurts done to them also are not to be much regarded. Of that, therefore, which we have not the smallest need to seek after, because the Lord did not seek after it either, we ought to endure without heart-sickness the cutting down or taking away. "Covetousness," the Spirit of the Lord has through the apostle pronounced "a root of all evils."[9087] Let us not interpret that covetousness as consisting merely in the concupiscence of what is another's: for even what seems ours is another's; for nothing is ours, since all things are God's, whose are we also ourselves. And so, if, when suffering from a loss, we feel impatiently, grieving for what is lost from what is not our own, we shall be detected as bordering on covetousness:

we seek what is another's when we ill brook losing what is another's. He who is greatly stirred with impatience of a loss, does, by giving things earthly the precedence over things heavenly, sin directly[9088] against God; for the Spirit, which he has received from the Lord, he greatly shocks for the sake of a worldly matter. Willingly, therefore, let us lose things earthly, let us keep things heavenly. Perish the whole world, [9089] so I may make patience my gain! In truth, I know not whether he who has not made up his mind to endure with constancy the loss of somewhat of his, either by theft, or else by force, or else even by carelessness, would himself readily or heartily lay hand on his own property in the cause of almsgiving:

for who that endures not at all to be cut by another, himself draws the sword on his own body? Patience in losses is an exercise in bestowing and communicating. Who fears not to lose, finds it not irksome to give. Else how will one, when he has two coats, give the one of them to the naked,[9090] unless he be a man likewise to offer to one who takes away his coat his cloak as well?[9091] How shall we fashion to us friends from mammon, [9092] if we love it so much as not to put up with its loss? We shall perish together with the lost mammon.

Why do we find here, where it is our business to lose? [9093] To exhibit impatience at all losses is the Gentiles' business, who give money the precedence perhaps over their soul; for so they do, when, in their cupidities of lucre, they encounter the gainful perils of commerce on the sea; when, for money's sake, even in the forum, there is nothing which damnation (itself) would fear which they hesitate to essay; when they hire themselves for sport and the camp; when, after the manner of wild beasts, they play the bandit along the highway. But us, according to the diversity by which we are distinguished from them, it becomes to lay down not our soul for money, but money for our soul, whether spontaneously in bestowing or patiently in losing.

Chapter VIII - Of Patience Under Personal Violence and Malediction

We who carry about our very soul, our very body, exposed in this world [9094] to injury from all, and exhibit patience under that injury; shall we be hurt at the loss [9095] of less important things?[9096] Far from a servant of Christ be such a defilement as that the patience which has been prepared for greater temptations should forsake him in frivolous ones. If one attempt to provoke you by manual violence, the monition of the Lord is at hand: "To him," He saith, "who smiteth thee on the face, turn the other cheek likewise." [9097] Let outrageousness [9098] be wearied out by your patience.

Whatever that blow may be, conjoined [9099] with pain and contumely, it [9100] shall receive a heavier one from the Lord.

You wound that outrageous [9101] one more by enduring: for he will be beaten by Him for whose sake you endure. If the tongue's bitterness break out in malediction or reproach, look back at the saying, "When they curse you, rejoice." [9102] The Lord Himself was "cursed" in the eye of the law;[9103] and yet is He the only Blessed One. Let us servants, therefore, follow our Lord closely; and be cursed patiently, that we may be able to be blessed. If I hear with too little equanimity some wanton or wicked word uttered against me, I must of necessity either myself retaliate the bitterness, or else I shall be racked with mute impatience. When, then, on being cursed, I smite (with my tongue,) how shall I be found to have followed the doctrine of the Lord, in which it has been delivered that "a man is defiled, [9104] not by the defilements of vessels, but of the things which are sent forth out of his mouth." Again, it is said that "impeachment [9105] awaits us for every vain and needless word." [9106] It follows that, from whatever the Lord keeps us, the same He admonishes us to bear patiently from another. I will add (somewhat) touching the pleasure of patience. For every injury, whether inflicted by tongue or hand, when it has lighted upon patience, will be dismissed [9107] with the same fate as, some weapon launched against and blunted on a rock of most stedfast hardness. For it will wholly fall then and there with bootless and fruitless labour; and sometimes will recoil and spend its rage on him who sent it out, with retorted impetus. No doubt the reason why any one hurts you is that you may be pained; because the hurter's enjoyment consists in the pain of the hurt. When, then, you have upset his enjoyment by not being pained, he must needs he pained by the loss of his enjoyment. Then you not only go unhurt away, which even alone is enough for you; but gratified, into the bargain, by your adversary's disappointment, and revenged by his pain.

This is the utility and the pleasure of patience.

Chapter IX - Of Patience Under Bereavement

Not even that species of impatience under the loss of our dear ones is excused, where some assertion of a right to grief acts the patron to it.

For the consideration of the apostle's declaration must be set before us, who says, "Be not overwhelmed with sadness at the falling asleep of any one, just as the nations are who are without hope."[9108] And justly; or, believing the resurrection of Christ we believe also in our own, for whose sake He both died and rose again. Since, then, there is certainty as to the resurrection of the dead, grief for death is needless, and impatience of grief is needless. For why should you grieve, if you believe that (your loved one) is not perished? Why should you bear impatiently the temporary withdrawal of him who you believe will return?

That which you think to be death is departure. He who goes before us is not to be lamented, though by all means to be longed for. [9109] That longing also must be tempered with patience. For why should you bear without moderation the fact that one is gone away whom you will presently follow?

Besides, impatience in matters of this kind bodes ill for our hope, and is a dealing insincerely with the faith.

And we wound Christ when we accept not with equanimity the summoning out of this world of any by Him, as if they were to be pitied. "I desire," says the apostle, "to be now received, and to be with Christ." [9110] How far better a desire does he exhibit! If, then, we grieve impatiently over such as have attained the desire of Christians, we show unwillingness ourselves to attain it.

Chapter X - Of Revenge

There is, too, another chief spur of impatience, the lust of revenge, dealing with the business either of glory or else of malice. But "glory," on the one hand, is everywhere "vain;" [9111] and malice, on the other, is always [9112] odious most of all, when, in this case indeed most of all, being provoked by a neighbour's malice, it constitutes itself superior [9113] in following out revenge, and by paying wickedness doubles that which has once been done. Revenge, in the estimation of error, [9114] seems a solace of pain; in the estimation of truth, on the contrary, it is convicted of malignity. For what difference is there between provoker and provoked, except that the former is detected as prior in evil-doing, but the latter as posterior? Yet each stands impeached of hurting a man in the eye of the Lord, who both prohibits and condemns every wickedness. In evil doing there is no account taken of order, nor does place separate what similarity conjoins. And the precept is absolute, that evil is not to be repaid with evil. [9115] Like deed involves like merit. How shall we observe that principle, if in our loathing [9116] we shall not loathe revenge? What honour, moreover, shall we be offering to the Lord God, if we arrogate to ourselves the arbitrament of vengeance? We are corrupt[9117] --earthen vessels. [9118] With our own servant-boys, [9119] if they assume to themselves the right of vengeance on their fellow-servants, we are gravely offended; while such as make us the offering of their patience we not only approve as mindful of humility, of servitude, affectionately jealous of the right of their lord's honour; but we make them an ampler satisfaction than they would have pre-exacted [9120] for themselves. Is there any risk of a different result in the case of a Lord so just in estimating, so potent in executing? Why, then, do we believe Him a Judge, if not an Avenger too? This He promises that He will be to us in return, saying, "Vengeance belongeth to me, and I will avenge;" [9121] that is, Leave patience to me, and I will reward patience. For when He says, "Judge not, lest ye be judged," [9122] does He not require patience? For who will refrain from judging another, but he who shall be patient in not revenging himself? Who judges in order to pardon? And if he shall pardon, still he has taken care to indulge the impatience of a judger, and has taken away the honour of the one Judge, that is, God. How many mischances had impatience of this kind been wont to run into! How oft has it repented of its revenge! How oft has its vehemence been found worse than the causes which led to it!--inasmuch as nothing undertaken with impatience can be effected without impetuosity:

nothing done with impetuosity fails either to stumble, or else to fall altogether, or else to vanish headlong.

Moreover, if you avenge yourself too slightly, you will be mad; if too amply, you will have to bear the burden. [9123] What have I to do with vengeance, the measure of which, through impatience of pain, I am unable to regulate? Whereas, if I shall repose on patience, I shall not feel pain; if I shall not feel pain, I shall not desire to avenge myself.

Chapter XI - Further Reasons for Practising Patience. Its Connection with the Beatitudes

After these principal material causes of impatience, registered to the best of our ability, why should we wander out of our way among the rest,--what are found at home, what abroad? Wide and diffusive is the Evil One's operation, hurling manifold irritations of our spirit, and sometimes trifling ones, sometimes very great. But the trifling ones you may contemn from their very littleness; to the very great ones you may yield in regard of their overpoweringness. Where the injury is less, there is no necessity for impatience; but where the injury is greater, there more necessary is the remedy for the injury--patience. Let us strive, therefore, to endure the inflictions of the Evil One, that the counter-zeal of our equanimity may mock the zeal of the foe. If, however, we ourselves, either by imprudence or else voluntarily, draw upon ourselves anything, let us meet with equal patience what we have to blame ourselves for. Moreover, if we believe that some inflictions are sent on us by the Lord, to whom should we more exhibit patience than to the Lord? Nay, He teaches [9124] us to give thanks and rejoice, over and above, at being thought worthy of divine chastisement. "Whom I love," saith He, "I chasten." [9125] O blessed servant, on whose amendment the Lord is intent! with whom He deigns to be wroth! whom He does not deceive by dissembling His reproofs! On every side, therefore, we are bound to the duty of exercising patience, from whatever quarter, either by our own errors or else by the snares of the Evil One, we incur the Lord's reproofs. Of that duty great is the reward--namely, happiness.

For whom but the patient has the Lord called happy, in saying, "Blessed are the poor in spirit, for theirs is the kingdom of the heavens?" [9126] No one, assuredly, is "poor in spirit," except he be humble. Well, who is humble, except he be patient? For no one can abase himself without patience, in the first instance, to bear the act of abasement. "Blessed," saith He, "are the weepers and mourners." [9127] Who, without patience, is tolerant of such unhappinesses? And so to such, "consolation" and "laughter" are promised.

"Blessed are the gentle:" [9128] under this term, surely, the impatient cannot possibly be classed. Again, when He marks "the peacemakers" [9129] with the same title of felicity, and names them "sons of God," pray have the impatient any affinity with "peace?"

Even a fool may perceive that.

When, however, He says, "Rejoice and exult, as often as they shall curse and persecute you; for very great is your reward in heaven," [9130] of course it is not to the impatience of exultation[9131] that He makes that promise; because no one will "exult" in adversities unless he have first learnt to contemn them; no one will contemn them unless he have learnt to practise patience.

Chapter XII - Certain Other Divine Precepts. The Apostolic Description of Charity. Their Connection with Patience

As regards the rule of peace, which [9132] is so pleasing to God, who in the world that is prone to impatience [9133] will even once forgive his brother, I will not say "seven times," or[9134] "seventy-seven times?" [9135] Who that is contemplating a suit against his adversary will compose the matter by agreement, [9136] unless he first begin by lopping off chagrin, hardheartedness, and bitterness, which are in fact the poisonous outgrowths of impatience? How will you "remit, and remission shall be granted" you [9137] if the absence of patience makes you tenacious of a wrong? No one who is at variance with his brother in his mind, will finish offering his "duteous gift at the altar," unless he first, with intent to "reconcile his brother," return to patience.[9138] If "the sun go down over our wrath," we are in jeopardy: [9139] we are not allowed to remain one day without patience. But, however, since Patience takes the lead in [9140] every species of salutary discipline, what wonder that she likewise ministers to Repentance, (accustomed as Repentance is to come to the rescue of such as have fallen,) when, on a disjunction of wedlock (for that cause, I mean, which makes it lawful, whether for husband or wife, to persist in the perpetual observance of widowhood), [9141] she [9142] waits for, she yearns for, she persuades by her entreaties, repentance in all who are one day to enter salvation? How great a blessing she confers on each!

The one she prevents from becoming an adulterer; the other she amends. So, too, she is found in those holy examples touching patience in the Lord's parables. The shepherd's patience seeks and finds the straying ewe: [9143] for Impatience would easily despise one ewe; but Patience undertakes the labour of the quest, and the patient burden-bearer carries home on his shoulders the forsaken sinner. [9144] That prodigal son also the father's patience receives, and clothes, and feeds, and makes excuses for, in the presence of the angry brother's impatience. [9145] He, therefore, who "had perished" is saved, because he entered on the way of repentance. Repentance perishes not, because it finds Patience (to welcome it).

For by whose teachings but those of Patience is Charity [9146] --the highest sacrament of the faith, the treasure-house of the Christian name, which the apostle commends with the whole strength of the Holy Spirit--trained? "Charity," he says, "is long suffering;" thus she applies patience: "is beneficent;" Patience does no evil: "is not emulous;" that certainly is a peculiar mark of patience:

"savours not of violence:" [9147] she has drawn her self-restraint from patience: "is not puffed up; is not violent;" [9148] for that pertains not unto patience:

"nor does she seek her own" if, she offers her own, provided she may benefit her neighbours: "nor is irritable;" if she were, what would she have left to Impatience? Accordingly he says, "Charity endures all things; tolerates all things;" of course because she is patient. Justly, then, "will she never fail;" [9149] for all other things will be cancelled, will have their consummation. "Tongues, sciences, prophecies, become exhausted; faith, hope, charity, are permanent:" Faith, which Christ's patience introduced; hope, which man's patience waits for; charity, which Patience accompanies, with God as Master.

Chapter XIII - Of Bodily Patience

Thus far, finally, of patience simple and uniform, and as it exists merely in the mind:

though in many forms likewise I labour after it in body, for the purpose of "winning the Lord;"[9150] inasmuch as it is a quality which has been exhibited by the Lord Himself in bodily virtue as well; if it is true that the ruling mind easily communicates the gifts [9151] of the Spirit with its bodily habitation. What, therefore, is the business of Patience in the body? In the first place, it is the affliction [9152] of the flesh--a victim [9153] able to appease the Lord by means of the sacrifice of humiliation--in making a libation to the Lord of sordid [9154] raiment, together with scantiness of food, content with simple diet and the pure drink of water [9155] in conjoining fasts to all this; in inuring herself to sackcloth and ashes.

This bodily patience adds a grace to our prayers for good, a strength to our prayers against evil; this opens the ears of Christ our God, [9156] dissipates severity, elicits clemency.

Thus that Babylonish king, [9157] after being exiled from human form in his seven years' squalor and neglect, because he had offended the Lord; by the bodily immolation of patience not only recovered his kingdom, but--what is more to be desired by a man--made satisfaction to God. Further, if we set down in order the higher and happier grades of bodily patience, (we find that) it is she who is entrusted by holiness with the care of continence of the flesh: she keeps the widow,[9158] and sets on the virgin the seal [9159] and raises the self-made eunuch to the realms of heaven.[9160] That which springs from a virtue of the mind is perfected in the flesh; and, finally, by the patience of the flesh, does battle under persecution.

If flight press hard, the flesh wars with [9161] the inconvenience of flight; if imprisonment overtake[9162] us, the flesh (still was) in bonds, the flesh in the gyve, the flesh in solitude, [9163] and in that want of light, and in that patience of the world's misusage. [9164] When, however, it is led forth unto the final proof of happiness, [9165] unto the occasion of the second baptism, [9166] unto the act of ascending the divine seat, no patience is more needed there than bodily patience. If the "spirit is willing, but the flesh," without patience, "weak," [9167] where, save in patience, is the safety of the spirit, and of the flesh itself?

But when the Lord says this about the flesh, pronouncing it "weak," He shows what need there is of strengthening, it--that is by patience--to meet [9168] every preparation for subverting or punishing faith; that it may bear with all constancy stripes, fire, cross, beasts, sword; all which prophets and apostles, by enduring, conquered!

Chapter XIV - The Power of This Twofold Patience, the Spiritual and the Bodily. Exemplified in the Saints of Old

With this strength of patience, Esaias is cut asunder, and ceases not to speak concerning the Lord; Stephen is stoned, and prays for pardon to his foes. [9169] Oh, happy also he who met all the violence of the devil by the exertion of every species of patience! [9170] --whom neither the driving away of his cattle nor those riches of his in sheep, nor the sweeping away of his children in one swoop of ruin, nor, finally, the agony of his own body in (one universal) wound, estranged from the patience and the faith which he had plighted to the Lord; whom the devil smote with all his might in vain. For by all his pains he was not drawn away from his reverence for God; but he has been set up as an example and testimony to us, for the thorough accomplishment of patience as well in spirit as in flesh, as well in mind as in body; in order that we succumb neither to damages of our worldly goods, nor to losses of those who are dearest, nor even to bodily afflictions.

What a bier [9171] for the devil did God erect in the person of that hero! What a banner did He rear over the enemy of His glory, when, at every bitter message, that man uttered nothing out of his mouth but thanks to God, while he denounced his wife, now quite wearied with ills, and urging him to resort to crooked remedies! How did God smile, [9172] how was the evil one cut asunder,[9173] while Job with mighty equanimity kept scraping off [9174] the unclean overflow of his own ulcer, while he sportively replaced the vermin that brake out thence, in the same caves and feeding-places of his pitted flesh! And so, when all the darts of temptations had blunted themselves against the corslet and shield of his patience, that instrument [9175] of God's victory not only presently recovered from God the soundness of his body, but possessed in redoubled measure what he had lost. And if he had wished to have his children also restored, he might again have been called father; but he preferred to have them restored him "in that day." [9176] Such joy as that--secure so entirely concerning the Lord--he deferred; meantime he endured a voluntary bereavement, that he might not live without some (exercise of) patience.

Chapter XV - General Summary of the Virtues and Effects of Patience

So amply sufficient a Depositary of patience is God. If it be a wrong which you deposit in His care, He is an Avenger; if a loss, He is a Restorer; if pain, He is a Healer; if death, He is a Reviver. What honour is granted to Patience, to have God as her Debtor! And not without reason: for she keeps all His decrees; she has to do with all His mandates. She fortifies faith; is the pilot of peace; assists charity; establishes humility; waits long for repentance; sets her seal on confession; rules the flesh; preserves the spirit; bridles the tongue; restrains the hand; tramples temptations under foot; drives away scandals; gives their crowning grace to martyrdoms; consoles the poor; teaches the rich moderation; overstrains not the weak; exhausts not the strong; is the delight of the believer; invites the Gentile; commends the servant to his lord, and his lord to God; adorns the woman; makes the man approved; is loved in childhood, praised in youth, looked up to in age; is beauteous in either sex, in every time of life. Come, now, see whether [9177] we have a general idea of her mien and habit.

Her countenance is tranquil and peaceful; her brow serene [9178] contracted by no wrinkle of sadness or of anger; her eyebrows evenly relaxed in gladsome wise, with eyes downcast in humility, not in unhappiness; her mouth sealed with the honourable mark of silence; her hue such as theirs who are without care and without guilt; the motion of her head frequent against the devil, and her laugh threatening; [9179] her clothing, moreover, about her bosom white and well fitted to her person, as being neither inflated nor disturbed.

For Patience sits on the throne of that calmest and gentlest Spirit, who is not found in the roll of the whirlwind, nor in the leaden hue of the cloud, but is of soft serenity, open and simple, whom Elias saw at his third essay. [9180] For where God is, there too is His foster-child, namely Patience. When God's Spirit descends, then Patience accompanies Him indivisibly. If we do not give admission to her together with the Spirit, will (He) always tarry with us? Nay, I know not whether He would remain any longer. Without His companion and handmaid, He must of necessity be straitened in every place and at every time. Whatever blow His enemy may inflict He will be unable to endure alone, being without the instrumental means of enduring.

Chapter XVI - The Patience of the Heathen Very Different from Christian Patience. Theirs Doomed to Perdition. Ours Destined to Salvation

This is the rule, this the discipline, these the works of patience which is heavenly and true; that is, of Christian patience, not false and disgraceful, like as is that patience of the nations of the earth. For in order that in this also the devil might rival the Lord, he has as it were quite on a par (except that the very diversity of evil and good is exactly on a par with their magnitude [9181]) taught his disciples also a patience of his own; that, I mean, which, making husbands venal for dowry, and teaching them to trade in panderings, makes them subject to the power of their wives; which, with feigned affection, undergoes every toil of forced complaisance, [9182] with a view to ensnaring the childless; [9183] which makes the slaves of the belly [9184] submit to contumelious patronage, in the subjection of their liberty to their gullet. Such pursuits of patience the Gentiles are acquainted with; and they eagerly seize a name of so great goodness to apply it to foul practises:

patient they live of rivals, and of the rich, and of such as give them invitations; impatient of God alone. But let their own and their leader's patience look to itself--a patience which the subterraneous fire awaits! Let us, on the other hand, love the patience of God, the patience of Christ; let us repay to Him the patience which He has paid down for us! Let us offer to Him the patience of the spirit, the patience of the flesh, believing as we do in the resurrection of flesh and spirit.

Elucidations

I.

(Unless patience sit by his side, cap. i)

Let me quote words which, many years ago, struck me forcibly, and which I trust, have been blest to my soul; for which reason, I must be allowed, here, to thank their author, the learned and fearless Dean Burgon, of Chichester. In his invaluable Commentary on the Gospel, which while it abounds in the fruits of a varied erudition, aims only to be practically useful, this pious scholar remarks: "To Faith must be added Patience, the patient waiting for God,' if we would escape the snare which Satan spread, no less for the Holy One (i.e. in the Temp. upon the Pinnacle) than for the Israelites at Massah. And this is perhaps the reason of the remarkable prominence given to the grace of Patience, both by our Lord and His Apostles; a circumstance, as it may be thought, which has not altogether attracted the attention which it deserves." He then cites examples; [9185] but a reference to any good concordance will strikingly exemplify the admirable comment of this "godly and well-learned man."

See his comments on Matt. iv. 7 and Luke xxi. 19.

II.

(Under their chin, cap. iv)

The reference in the note to Paris, as represented by Virgil and in ancient sculpture, seems somewhat to the point:

"Et nunc ille Paris, cum semiviro comitatu.

Mæonia mentum mitra crinemq, madentem,

Subnixus, etc."

He had just spoken of the pileus as a "Cap of freedom," but there was another form of pileus which was just the reverse and was probably tied by fimbriæ, under the chin, denoting a low order of slaves, effeminate men, perhaps spadones. Now, the Phrygian bonnet to which Virgil refers, is introduced by him to complete the reproach of his contemptuous expression (semiviro comitatu) just before.

So, our author--"not only from men, i.e. men so degraded as to wear this badge of extreme servitude, but even from cattle, etc. Shall these mean creatures outdo us in obedience and patience?"

III.

(The world's misusage, cap. xiii)

The Reverend Clergy who may read this note will forgive a brother, who begins to be in respect of years, like "Paul the aged," for remarking, that the reading of the Ante-Nicene Fathers often leads him to sigh--"Such were they from whom we have received all that makes life tolerable, but how intolerable it was for them: are we, indeed, such as they would have considered Christians?" God be praised for His mercy and forbearance in our days; but, still it is true that "we have need of patience." Is not much of all that we regard as "the world's misusage," the gracious hand of the Master upon us, giving us something for the exercise of that Patience, by which He forms us into His own image? (Heb. xii. 3.) Impatience of obscurity, of poverty, of ingratitude, of misrepresentation, of "the slings and arrows" of slander and abuse, is a revolt against that indispensable discipline of the Gospel which requires us to "endure afflictions" in some form or other. Who can complain when one thinks what it would have cost us to be Christians in Tertullian's time? The ambition of the Clergy is always rebellion against God, and "patient waiting" is its only remedy. One will find profitable reading on this subject in Massillon, [9186] de l'Ambition des Clercs: "Reposez-vous sur le Seigneur du soin de votre destinée: il saura bien accomplir, tout seul, les desseins qu'il a sur vous. Si votre élévation est son bon plaisir, elle sera, aussi son ouvrage. Rendez-vous ἐv digne seulement par la retraite, par la frayeur, par la fuite, par les sentiments vifs de votre indignité...c'est ainsi que les Chrysostome, les Grégoire, les Basil, les Augustin, furent donnés à l'Église."

Footnotes:

9013. [Written possibly as late as a.d. 202; and is credited by Neander and Kaye, with Catholic Orthodoxy.]

9014. "Nullius boni;" compare Rom. vii. 18.

9015. [Elucidation I.]

9016. i.e. who arc strangers to it.

9017. Or, "striving after."

9018. Or, "heathendom"--sæculi.

9019. Sæculo.

9020. i.e. us Christians.

9021. i.e. cynical = κυνικός = doglike. But Tertullian appears to use "caninæ" purposely, and I have therefore retained it rather than substitute (as Mr. Dodgson does) "cynical."

9022. i.e. the affectation is modelled by insensibility.

9023. See Ps. lxxiv. 23 in A.V. It is Ps. lxxiii. in the LXX.

9024. Because they see no visible proof of it.

9025. Sæculo.

9026. So Mr. Dodgson; and La Cerda, as quoted by Oehler. See Ps. cxxxi. 1 in LXX., where it is Ps. cxxx.

9027. 1 John i. 1.

9028. I have followed Oehler's reading of this very difficult and much disputed passage. For the expression, "having been trained," etc., compare Heb. v. 8.

9029. Luke ix. 51-56.

9030. Or, "yet had there been need of contumelies likewise for the undergoing of death?"

9031. "Obsequium," distinguished by Döderlein from "obedientia," as a more voluntary and spontaneous thing, founded less on authority than respect and love.

9032. Obsequii.

9033. "Pollicetur," not "promittit."

9034. Obedientiam.

9035. "Subnixis." Perhaps this may be the meaning, as in Virg. Æn. iv. 217. But

Oehler notices "subnexis" as a conjecture of Jos. Scaliger, which is very plausible, and would mean nearly the same. Mr. Dodgson renders "supported by their slavery;" and Oehler makes "subnixis" ="præditis," "instructis." [Elucidation II.]

9036. Obsequii.

9037. Pecudibus," i.e. tame domestic cattle.

9038. "Bestiis," irrational creatures, as opposed to "homines," here apparently wild beasts.

9039. Obsequii. For the sentiment, compare Isa. i. 3.

9040. Obsequii.

9041. See above, "the creatures...acknowledge their masters."

9042. Obsequio.

9043. Obsequio.

9044. "Oblectatur" Oehler reads with the mss.

The editors, as he says, have emended "Obluctatur," which Mr. Dodgson reads.

9045. See the previous chapter.

9046. See the previous chapter.

9047. See chap. i.

9048. [All our author's instances of this principle of the Præscriptio are noteworthy, as interpreting its use in the Advs. Hæreses.]

9049. "Procedere:" so Oehler, who, however, notices an ingenious conjecture of Jos. Scaliger--"procudere," the hammering out, or forging.

9050. Tertullian may perhaps wish to imply, in prayer. See Matt. vi. 7.

9051. Facere. But Fulv. Ursinus (as Oehler tells us) has suggested a neat emendation--"favere," favours.

9052. See Ps. viii. 4-6.

9053. Compare the expression in de Idol. iv., "perdition of blood" ="bloody perdition," and the note there.

So here "angel of perdition" may ="lost angel."

9054. Mulier. See de Orat. c. xxii.

9055. 1 Cor. vii. 3; compare also 1 Pet. iii. 7.

9056. Impetu.

9057. Colonus. Gen. ii. 15.

9058. Sapere. See de Idol. c. i. sub fin.

9059. Homo.

9060. Matrix. Mr. Dodgson renders womb, which is admissible; but the other passages quoted by Oehler, where Tertullian uses this word, seem to suit better with the rendering given in the text.

9061. Compare a similar expression in de Idol. ii. ad init.

9062. Which Tertullian has just shown to be the result of impatience.

9063. i.e. murder.

9064. i.e. unable to restrain.

9065. i.e. want of power or patience to contemn gain.

9066. "Ordinatur;" but "orditur" has been very plausibly conjectured.

9067. Mr. Dodgson refers to ad Uxor. i. 5, q. v. sub fin.

9068. Or, "unduteous of duteousness."

9069. i.e. impatient.

9070. I have departed slightly here from Oehler's punctuation.

9071. Ex. xxxii. 1; Acts vii. 39, 40.

9072. i.e. the water which followed them, after being given forth by the smitten rock. See 1 Cor. x. 4.

9073. See Num. xx. 1-6. But Tertullian has apparently confused this with Ex. xv. 22, which seems to be the only place where "a three-days' thirst" is mentioned.

9074. Free, i.e. from the bondage of impatience and of sin.

9075. See Gen. xv. 6; Rom. iv. 3, 9, 22; Gal. iii. 6; James ii. 23.

9076. i.e. the trial was necessary not to prove his faith to God, who knows all whom He accounts righteous, but "typically" to us.

9077. Gal. iii. 16.

9078. John i. 17; Rom. vi. 14, 15.

9079. Matt. vi. 38, and the references there given.

9080. Composuit.

9081. See Matt. v. 22; and Wordsworth in loco, who thinks it probable that the meaning is "apostate."

9082. Ps. cxl. 3; Rom. iii. 13; James iii. 8.

9083. Matt. v. 44, 45.

9084. Sæculo.

9085. Subjacet.

9086. This appears to be the sense of this very difficult passage as Oehler reads it; and of Fr. Junius' interpretation of it, which Oehler approves.

9087. 1 Tim. vi. 10. See de Idol. xi. ad init.

9088. De proximo. See above, c. v. Deo de proximo amicus, "a most intimate friend to God."

9089. Sæculum.

9090. Luke iii. 11.

9091. Matt. v. 40; Luke vi. 29.

9092. Luke xvi. 9.

9093. "Alluding to Christ's words in Matt. x. 39" (Rigalt. quoted by Oehler).

9094. Sæculo.

9095. Delibatione.

9096. i.e. money and the like. Compare Matt. vi. 25; Luke xii. 23.

9097. Matt. v. 39.

9098. Improbitas.

9099. Constrictus. I have rendered after Oehler: but may not the meaning be "clenched," like the hand which deals the blow?

9100. As Oehler says "the blow" is said to "receive" that which, strictly, the dealer of it receives.

9101. Improbum.

9102. Matt. v. 11, 12; Luke vi. 22, 23.

9103. Deut. xxi. 23; Gal. iii. 13. Tertullian's quotations here are somewhat loose. He renders words which are distinct in the Greek by the same in his Latin.

9104. Communicari--κοινοῦσθαι. See Mark vii. 15, "made common," i.e. profane, unclean. Compare Acts x. 14, 15 in the Greek.

9105. Reatum. See de Idol. i. ad init., "the highest impeachment of the age."

9106. Matt. xii. 36. Tertullian has rendered ἀργόν by "vani et supervacui."

9107. Dispungetur: a word which, in the active, means technically "to balance accounts," hence "to discharge," etc.

9108. 1 Thess. iv. 13, not very strictly rendered.

9109. Desiderandus.

9110. Phil. i. 23, again loosely rendered: e.g. ἀναλῦσαι ="to weigh anchor," is rendered by Tertullian "recipi."

9111. See Gal. v. 26; Phil. ii. 3.

9112. Nunquam non.

9113. i.e. perhaps superior in degree of malice.

9114. i.e. of the world and its erroneous philosophies.

9115. Rom. xii. 17.

9116. Fastidientes, i.e. our loathing or abhorrence of sin. Perhaps the reference may be to Rom. xii. 9.

9117. Isa. lxiv. 6.

9118. Isa. lxiv. 8; 2 Cor. iv. 7.

9119. Servulis.

9120. Præsumpsissent.

9121. Deut. xxxii. 35; Ps. xciv. 1;

Rom. xii. 19; Heb. x. 30.

9122. Matt. vii. 1; Luke vi. 37.

9123. i.e. the penalty which the law will inflict.

9124. Docet. But a plausible conjecture, "decet," "it becomes us," has been made.

9125. Prov. iii. 11, 12; Heb. xii. 5, 6; Rev. iii. 19.

9126. Matt. v. 3.

9127. Matt. v. 4.

9128. Matt. v. 5.

9129. Matt. v. 9.

9130. Matt. v. 11, 12, inexactly quoted.

9131. Exultationis impatientiæ.

9132. i.e. peace.

9133. Impatientiæ natus: lit. "born for impatience." Comp. de Pæniten. 12, ad fin. "nec ulli rei nisi pænitentiæ natus."

9134. Oehler reads "sed," but the "vel" adopted in the text is a conjecture of Latinius, which Oehler mentions.

9135. Septuagies septies. The reference is to Matt. xviii. 21, 22. Compare de Orat. vii. ad fin. and the note there.

9136. Matt. v. 25.

9137. Luke vi. 37.

9138. Matt. v. 23, 24.

9139. Eph. iv. 26. Compare de Orat. xi.

9140. Gubernet.

9141. What the cause is is disputed. Opinions are divided as to whether Tertullian means by it "marriage with a heathen" (which as Mr. Dodgson reminds us, Tertullian--de Uxor. ii. 3--calls "adultery"), or the case in which our Lord allowed divorce.

See Matt. xix. 9.

9142. i.e. patience.

9143. Luke xv. 3-6.

9144. Peccatricem, i.e. the ewe.

9145. Luke xv. 11-32.

9146. Dilectio = ἀγάπη. See Trench, New Testament Syn., s. v. ἀγάπη; and with the rest of this chapter compare carefully, in the Greek, 1 Cor. xiii. [Neander points out the different view our author takes of the same parable, in the de Pudicit. cap. 9, Vol. IV. this series.]

9147. Protervum = Greek περπερεύεται.

9148. Proterit = Greek ἀσχημονεῖ.

9149. Excidet = Greek ἐκλείπει, suffers eclipse.

9150. Phil. iii. 8.

9151. "Invecta," generally = "movables", household furniture.

9152. Or, mortification, "adflictatio."

9153. i.e. fleshly mortification is a "victim," etc.

9154. Or, "mourning." Comp. de Pæn. c. 9.

9155. [The "water vs. wine" movement is not a discovery of our own times. "Drink a little wine," said St. Paul medicinally; but (as a great and good divine once remarked) "we must not lay stress on the noun, but the adjective; let it be very little."]

9156. Christi dei.

9157. Dan. iv. 33-37. Comp. de Pæn. c. 12. [I have removed an ambiguity by slightly touching the text here.]

9158. 1 Tim. v. 3, 9, 10; 1 Cor. vii. 39, 40.

9159. 1 Cor. vii. 34, 35.

9160. Matt. xix. 12.

9161. Ad. It seems to mean flesh has strength given it, by patience, to meet the hardships of the flight. Compare the πρὸς πλησμονὴν τῆς σαρκὸς, of St. Paul in Col. ii. 23. [Kaye compares this with the De Fuga, as proof of the author's freedom from Montanism, when this was written.]

9162. Præveniat: "prevent" us, before we have time to flee.

9163. Solo.

9164. [Elucidation III.]

9165. i.e. martyrdom.

9166. Comp. Luke xii. 50.

9167. Matt. xxvi. 41.

9168. "Adversus," like the "ad" above, note 21, p. 713.

9169. Acts vii. 59, 60.

9170. Job. See Job i. and ii.

9171. "Feretrum"--for carrying trophies in a triumph, the bodies of the dead, and their effigies, etc.

9172. Compare Ps. ii. 4.

9173. i.e. with rage and disappointment.

9174. Job ii. 8.

9175. Operarius.

9176. See 2 Tim. iv. 8. There is no authority for this statement of Tertullian's in Scripture. [It is his inference rather.]

9177. Si. This is Oehler's reading, who takes "si" to be ="an." But perhaps "sis" (="si vis"), which is Fr. Junius' correction, is better: "Come, now, let us, if you please, give a general sketch of her mien and habit."

9178. Pura; perhaps "smooth."

9179. Compare with this singular feature, Isa. xxxvii. 22.

9180. i.e., as Rigaltius (referred to by Oehler), explains, after the two visions of angels who appeared to him and said, "Arise and eat." See 1 Kings xix. 4-13. [It was the fourth, but our author having mentioned two, inadvertently calls it the third, referring to the "still small voice," in which Elijah saw His manifestation.]

9181. One is finite, the other infinite.

9182. Obsequii.

9183. And thus getting a place in their wills.

9184. i.e. professional "diners out." Comp. Phil. iii. 19.

9185. See--A Plain Commentary on the Four Gospels, intended chiefly for Devotional Reading. Oxford, 1854.

Also (Vol. I. p. 28) Philadelphia, 1855.

9186. OEuvres, Tom. vi. pp. 133-5. Ed. Paris, 1824.

www.ingramcontent.com/pod-product-compliance
Lightning Source LLC
Chambersburg PA
CBHW032107080426
42733CB00006B/450